GLORIA
BENEDICT ANDREWS

CURRENCY PRESS
SYDNEY

GRIFFIN
THEATRE
COMPANY

CURRENT THEATRE SERIES

First published in 2016
by Currency Press Pty Ltd,
PO Box 2287, Strawberry Hills, NSW, 2012, Australia
enquiries@currency.com.au
www.currency.com.au

in association with Griffin Theatre Company

Cataloguing-in-publication data for this title is available from the National Library of Australia website: www.nla.gov.au

Typeset by Dean Nottle for Currency Press.
Printed by Fineline Print + Copy Services, St Peters, NSW.
Front cover shows Marta Dusseldorp.
Cover photograph by Brett Boardman.
Cover design by RE:.

Contents

Gloria was first produced by Griffin Theatre Company at SBW Stables Theatre, Sydney, on 26 August 2016, with the following cast:

MADDIE / GIRL	Chloe Bayliss
CASSIE / WOMAN	Kristy Best
GLORIA	Marta Dusseldorp
PAUL	Louis Fontaine / Max Philips
DEREK / MAN	Huw Higginson
CLIENT / MAN 2 / KIP / ASSISTANT DIRECTOR	Pierce Wilcox
JARED	Meyne Wyatt

Director, Lee Lewis
Associate Director, Ben Winspear
Designer, Sophie Fletcher
Lighting Designer, Luiz Pampolha
Audio Visual Designer, Toby Knyvett
Composer, Steve Toulmin
Photographer and Videographer, Brett Boardman
Stage Manager, Natalie Moir
Production Coordinator, Danny Oliver
Child Chaperone, Elishia Semaan

CHARACTERS

GLORIA, late 40s

JARED, teenager, then 20s

DEREK / MAN, 40-something

MADDIE / GIRL, 12

CASSIE / WOMAN, mid-20s

PAUL, 6 or 7

CLIENT / MAN 2 / KIP / ASSISTANT DIRECTOR, around 30

This play went to press before the end of rehearsals and may differ from the play as performed.

ONE

Living room. Night. A woman sits watching TV. Sound on mute. A small boy beside her. He might be a doll. Or not. Nothing for a while. The woman walks to the kitchen, opens the fridge, stares inside. Finally, she pours a glass of milk which the boy drinks, still watching the television. When he's finished, she rinses the glass and puts it in the dishwasher. She takes a kitchen knife from the drawer and sits beside the boy. He snuggles into her and she strokes his hair. They watch television. The woman cradles the boy. She kisses his head. Stares at the television. A sound like all the air being sucked from a room. TV flickering.

Black.

1

The apartment.

JARED: At night when I can't sleep, I walk through the rooms. Feet quiet on the carpet. The refrigerator hums. Our house is a stage set and I'm the only living character. The others are puppets. Made of wood, cloth and porcelain. Faces painted on. They lie in their beds, attached to strings, snoring, mumbling, farting, until the string jerks and up they get to play their parts. That weird glow. Is it moonlight? Or glare from the city? Don't care anymore. I walk the halls. Open fridge. Drink juice. Pick at leftovers. Not hungry but do it anyway. All that stuff in plastic and foil. Half-eaten. Cold. Balcony. The city lights stop where the sea begins. Points of orange float in the black. Freighters anchored offshore. Out there I'd sleep. On a bunk. In a cabin. Rocked by swell. One day I'll leave and see the world by ship. I'll work hard, and when day is done, the throbbing of the engines will comfort my sleep. Down in the hull. Cocooned. I walk through our cold, blue rooms. I'm the only real character. The others are puppets. Jerking in their sleep. Derek dribbles into his pillow. Snores. Like a tractor dragging machinery. How can she stand it? Her porcelain face on the pillow. Kiss her sleeping eyes. They open. Stare. We're statues. No. We're actors on the far side of the curtain, listening for the audience. That hum. We dare not move. The curtain billows. Her eyes click shut. She rolls over. On her strings. I walk the silent rooms. Headphones. Computer. I'm a sniper taking out targets. Get a position on the roof, zoom in on a target. I place the shots where I like. Head or body. Leg if I want them to fall first. So I don't get bored. So each kill doesn't feel the same. Or porn. The clips where the girls talk to the camera as if the camera is you. I prefer this. When they're pretending to be with just me, not some guy or girl or gangbang. She talks to me as if I'm in the room with her. In front of her on the grey carpet. Crawling toward the sofa where she rips holes in her stockings. Teasing me about how I can't touch her, can't *really touch* her. *Bet you wish you could touch this perfect little pussy*. But she's wrong. I don't want that. I just want to watch her contort on the sofa until I fall asleep. I'll play the game or watch the girl until I'm asleep. Soon we'll wake, begin the day, play our parts. The house is quiet. Listen. This is how our house sounds at night—

Silence.

2

Living room.

GLORIA: He won't wake up.
DEREK: What?
GLORIA: I called him.
DEREK: Doesn't he have school?
GLORIA: It's a holiday.
DEREK: What for?
GLORIA: I don't know. A study break.
DEREK: So. He's sleeping in. Taking a break.

He laughs a bit too hard.

GLORIA: I called and called. Went in and shook him but he won't wake up.
DEREK: You shook him?
GLORIA: I said, wake up darling, *uppies tuppies.* And yes gently shook him. But he's out cold. Dribbling into his pillow. Headphones on. Why don't you try?

DEREK: Me?
GLORIA: He shouldn't let the day go to waste.
DEREK: Let him sleep. He's a growing boy.
GLORIA: Sleeping all day won't help him.
DEREK: Gives us time. Alone. We never.
GLORIA: Derek, he's sleeping. In the next.
DEREK: Please baby.
GLORIA: He could wake any. And Maddie.
DEREK: Gloria. Please. We.
GLORIA: Not now.
DEREK: So beautiful.
GLORIA: Another.
DEREK: I want a child.

Pause.

With you.
GLORIA: It's not the right.
DEREK: Of our own.
GLORIA: We've been through this.
DEREK: Our child.

JARED *enters.*

GLORIA: Breakfast is cold.
JARED: Not hungry. Anyway don't like eggs.
GLORIA: Since when? You always.
JARED: They're slimy.
DEREK: So. Big study day today.
JARED: Big what?
DEREK: Study.
JARED: I'm going out.
GLORIA: Where?
JARED: Out.
GLORIA: Who with?
JARED: You don't know them.
DEREK: What about study?
GLORIA: Leave it, Derek.
JARED: Yeah, Derek. What kind of a name is Derek anyway?
DEREK: A name. It's my name.

JARED: Derek. What does that even mean?

DEREK: You really want to know?

JARED: Enlighten me, Derek.

DEREK: It's Old German actually.

JARED: No shit.

DEREK: Theodoric. Ruler of the tribe.

JARED: All hail Theo*dork*.

GLORIA: I watch them. My two beautiful men.

JARED: Who gives someone a name like that? *Derek*.

DEREK: My parents. Did. Obviously.

JARED: You're seriously cracking me up, Derek.

GLORIA: My son laughs. Opens the fridge. Picks at leftovers. Drinks juice. When he was little, just the two of us and I was always working, he'd come to rehearsals. Sit in the corner and watch. Very quiet. Rapt. Sometimes the scene we were rehearsing was too *full-on*—you know too violent or sex—so he'd go off into the green room with one of the assistants. I didn't realise—of course it was obvious—how much he wanted to watch those scenes, especially those scenes. He gave the assistant the slip, snuck in. I didn't realise. Too *in the moment*. He crouched in the shadows. Watched Mummy play some full-on scene. Drenched with gore. Butchered. Or having sex. [*Laughs.*] Naked on the floor going for it you know. All these people watching, taking notes. And him, under a table or behind some scenery—hot little eyes on me—while I feigned pleasure, ecstasy, over and over. What was that like for him? Watching that. What does he remember? God.

Pause.

Whenever I perform these days—which is less and less—he comes to the dress rehearsal and after we talk about what he liked or didn't, what he *got*, what he thought the production—the director—was trying to achieve. He has strong opinions and I like that. Notices things. Details. But he doesn't come to rehearsals anymore. Prefers to do his own thing, hang out with friends.

Pause.

I remember his eyes. In the dark. I play the scene for those eyes.

MADDIE *enters. Dressed like a princess.*

MADDIE: Hiya.

GLORIA: Hi darling.

Silence. MADDIE *goes to* DEREK. *He runs his fingers through her hair.*

Beyond the sliding glass doors, Derek leans on the balcony. His daughter takes his hand. They look to the horizon. Ships in the bay, the blue. He ruffles her hair. I'm alone at the table with my son's plate of untouched eggs. A breeze blows through the open doors. Through our rooms.

3

Balcony.

MADDIE: Are you're going away again?
DEREK: Just a short trip.
MADDIE: Where to?
DEREK: Singapore.
MADDIE: Can I come?
DEREK: Sweetheart, you're staying here with Gloria. And Jared.
MADDIE: I want to come and eat breakfast with the orangutans.
DEREK: Another time. Promise.
MADDIE: I stand on tippy toes and look down. Everything's tiny.
DEREK: Long way down.
MADDIE: Do you ever feel like jumping?
DEREK: Jumping? Why? I love you and Gloria. And Jared. No way.
MADDIE: Sometimes it pops into my head that I could climb over.
DEREK: Sometimes everyone. High places. Balconies. Just something your brain. Irrational. But we don't do it.
MADDIE: What's irrational?
DEREK: The opposite of rational. You know. What makes us human. How we think. Logic. We don't give in to irrational impulses.
MADDIE: Like apes.
DEREK: What? Yes, like apes.
MADDIE: Or the orangutans. That's why I want to eat breakfast with them. To experience that. Are the orangutans in Singapore Zoo irrational?
DEREK: They're different from us, sweetheart. Different cognitive architecture.

MADDIE: So thoughts just pop into their heads too?
DEREK: No. Maybe. I don't.
MADDIE: What about Jared? Is he irrational?
DEREK: No. Well. Sometimes, we all can be sweetheart.
MADDIE: I don't want you to jump.

Pause.

Don't ever jump.
DEREK: I won't.
MADDIE: You'd splatter.

They look.

DEREK: Don't think about it.
MADDIE: I'm not.
DEREK: Good.

Silence. They watch a plane crossing the sky.

MADDIE: If you love us so much—me, Gloria and Jared—so much you don't want to throw yourself off the balcony and splatter—if that's true—why are you always leaving us?

He runs his fingers through her hair.

4

Bathroom.

Steam from the shower. JARED *stands in front of the mirror. He wipes condensation from the glass.*

JARED: I'm the only real character. The rest are puppets. I'm crawling toward you. I can hear you. Through the steam. Are you there?

5

Living room.

MADDIE *eats breakfast.* DEREK *pretends to be an orangutan. He takes it very seriously, tries to be as natural as possible.*

MADDIE: My dad's gone to Singapore. For work. I'm stuck here with his wife and her son. She's not my mummy and he's not my brother.

He gives me the total creeps. What about you? Do you ever wish you were back in the jungle? Do you miss your family?

Pause.

At least you get to eat really great breakfasts with people from all over the world. That must be fun for you. Or do you just pretend? You're doing a good job. You're convincing.

He smiles.

You've got an oversized bite. You should get that corrected. So you don't scare the clients. Like me. You wouldn't want that now would you?

Pause.

Do thoughts just pop into your head? Dad said orangutans have got different cognitive architecture. Like what? Mini condominiums with mini people eating miniature breakfasts in your brain? Or doing something *irrational* like—?

She makes a crazy face, speaks a phrase or two of gibberish.

Like Jared. Walking around the apartment at night. How's that rational? He stares at me. Why don't you say something? Do you miss the jungle? Sad old ape. Do you miss Mummy?

Pause.

More coffee?

She pours him more coffee. He stares at it.

Mummy's dead. I went to her funeral and threw dirt in her grave. I wore black and lace. Now we live up here.

Finally, he picks up the cup and takes a sip.

I don't think orangutans actually drink coffee. I don't think they're *allowed* to drink coffee.

Beat.

Better go pack, you don't want to miss your plane.

He finishes his coffee and leaves.

Shithead.

GLORIA *clears away the breakfast.*

6

Bathroom.

JARED: I know you're there. I can hear you. Through the steam.

7

Bathroom.

CASSIE *showers. Sings to herself. A dreamy pop song.*

8

Living room.

MADDIE *practises her routine.*

GLORIA: Getting good Maddie, really coming along.

She watches MADDIE *practise.*

What do you call this one? What's this routine, sweetheart?

MADDIE *messes up the routine, trips or tangles her ribbons.*

Sorry, I'm disturbing you.

MADDIE *continues her routine. Twirling.*

9

Bathroom.

CASSIE *is drying herself.* PAUL *watches her.*

CASSIE: Mummy needs to get ready, darling. Why don't you read a book or play your game. Let Mummy get ready.

Pause.

Please darling. Don't make me late.

10

Living room.

MADDIE *is still practising.*

MADDIE: It's just something I made up. From watching clips. You have to keep the ribbons moving. They're not allowed to stop. This is a *twirl* and this is a *spiral* and this is a *snake* and this is *loop-the-loop.* And look *flowers.* I want to get really good. Compete. I read a comment on one of the blogs and it inspired me, *you've got a dream, protect it, you want something, go get it.* I want to get out there and compete. Do you think Daddy will let me? He bought me the ribbons and the ball.

GLORIA: I don't know darling. We haven't discussed it.

MADDIE: But he bought the equipment.

GLORIA: You just need to discuss it with him. When he's back.

MADDIE: I want to see him. Show him my routine.

GLORIA: Soon.

MADDIE *stops.*

Why did you stop? Not because of me.

MADDIE: It's hard to talk and practise at the same time. Can't concentrate.

GLORIA: He'll be home any day now. I just spoke to him. He's good. Busy.

MADDIE: Did he eat breakfast with the orangutans?

GLORIA: I don't know sweetheart. He's busy.

11

Cassie's room.

She brushes her hair.

CASSIE: You okay darling? You're very quiet. Paul?

12

Living room.

PAUL *plays his video game.*

13

Living room.

DEREK: I'm in this service station all day. It's so boring.

GLORIA: What for?

DEREK: We're running in the new system on the computers. The sales staff have been re-trained and I'm there to keep an eye on things. Make sure there are no glitches. I'm desperate for something to go wrong so I've got something to do. How's Maddie?

GLORIA: Fine. She misses you. She's out on the balcony.

DEREK: On the balcony? Is she okay?

GLORIA: She's fine. Why?

DEREK: No reason.

GLORIA: Don't you trust me with her?

DEREK: I'm just bored. Nothing to do here but read magazines.

GLORIA: She's fine. Twirling her ribbon in the breeze.

Pause.

We miss you. We all miss you.

14

Cassie's room.

CASSIE: I put on my face. Sit at the mirror, paint on my eyes and my lips. Colour my cheeks. I'm always like this before a date. You know, butterflies. What am I in for?

15

Living room.

GLORIA: In my costume fitting today, Alice the costume designer said I had a *banging body*. She actually said that. *Babe, you've got a banging body.* I was trying on this sequin dress she wants me to wear in the fourth act. This real tight number. She said I was *hot*. I'm supposed to look seductive in the fourth act. *Really hot.* She was probably trying to make me feel better. The play, my body, my age. Rehearsals are hard. I worry about glitches in my performance.

DEREK: Glitches?

GLORIA: Like repeat a word by accident. Same thing twice without realising. Or blanks. Insert random blanks.

DEREK: I'm looking for glitches all the time.

GLORIA: I sound fake.

DEREK: All day long.

GLORIA: Do you think I'm fake?

DEREK: I sit behind the counter. A bit to the side. Turning the pages of a magazine. One eye on the transactions. Making sure the program is running alright. You're not fake.

GLORIA: I'm worried about the kids.

DEREK: I've got my own screen. Plugged into the main system. Where I monitor the transactions.

GLORIA: At rehearsals. I worry about the kids. Alone up here.

DEREK: The program. Running in. The kids are fine.

GLORIA: What if someone.

DEREK: It's totally safe. They're fine. Beep beep beep. All day long.

GLORIA: Is that why Alice said that about my body, because she can see I'm distracted? Not really inside the role. Fuck, is that why Alice said that?

DEREK: There's security. No-one gets in unless they belong. The hallways are monitored. Cameras. The door. It's fine.

GLORIA: You've got a banging body babe. What does that even mean?

DEREK *holds her. Kisses her neck.*

I miss you. I want you to hold me.

He runs his fingers through her hair.

I miss your touch. Your fingers through my hair.

He strips her or she strips herself. Hard to tell.

Why did she say that?

JARED: I'm going out Mum.

GLORIA: Where?

JARED: Out. With friends.

GLORIA: Be safe.

JARED: Don't worry Mum. Don't worry all the time.

JARED *leaves.*

GLORIA: When I was a little girl, there was a river—a secret river—running under the floor. I lived in my cellar. Footsteps on the ceiling. Dragging sounds. Feet, music. Like I was a princess in the turret of a castle and I could hear this faraway music—waltzes, foxtrots, the fandango—carried on the breeze from a magnificent ball where I was supposed to be. There was no ball. There were no windows, no turret. I was in my cellar. Where the walls were cold. Because of the river. Under the floor. Said Daddy. The river was *ancient*. It went right under our house. He saw it every day flowing through the city up there. I'd never been up there, never seen it. He said a real dirty river, polluted and foul. Once he saw a baby carriage floating in it. And another time in the dirty muck there was a rocking horse. Daddy had a solution. How to fix it. Dig a channel. *A whole other river*. Under the dirty river and take away the foul brown river muck. Then the river on top would be crystal clean and the citizens crossing the bridges or strolling along the banks wouldn't be disturbed by the muck anymore. Said Daddy. When they looked down from the bridges or riverbank, they wouldn't see rubbish and prams and dead animals—*all sorts of filth*—they'd see a clear sparkling river. They could even swim in it again. He said. Jesus. I'm cold. The breeze. I wish she'd close the door. Close the door darling. It's windy. Maddie, close the door. Please sweetheart close the door. Sweetheart?

16

Living room.

A knock at the door. CASSIE *lets* JARED *in.*

CASSIE: Hi. Welcome.

JARED: Hi.

CASSIE: Thanks for this.

JARED: Hey no problem, happy to help.

CASSIE: He'll watch TV or play his game then sleep. Shouldn't be too late. 'Bye sweetheart.

PAUL: 'Bye.

JARED: Have fun.

CASSIE: I'll try. You too. 'Bye.

JARED: Thanks. 'Bye.

CASSIE *leaves.*

Paul. Hi. I'm Jared.

17

Living room.

MADDIE: It's not 'once he saw a baby carriage floating in it'. It's just 'baby'. 'Once he saw a *baby* floating in it and a rocking horse.' The baby carriage—the pram—comes later. 'When they looked down into the river, they wouldn't see rubbish and prams and dead animals.' But the rest was good. You've pretty much got the whole speech down. Wanna do it again?

GLORIA: No thanks darling.

MADDIE: Are there really underground rivers?

GLORIA: I guess so. Under cities. When they build.

MADDIE: But not rivers under rivers. That's just an idea right?

GLORIA: Yes. Fantasy stuff.

MADDIE: So why is her house underground?

GLORIA: Her daddy built it for her.

MADDIE: Because he didn't want her to run away?

GLORIA: Because he wanted to keep her safe.

MADDIE: From what?

GLORIA: Harmful things.

MADDIE: Was she sad?

GLORIA: Sometimes everybody gets sad.

MADDIE: Do you get sad?

GLORIA: When I miss your dad. But he'll be back soon. Shall we watch something fun? The chefs. Or the dancing. You like that, right? Ball gowns.

18

Living room.

JARED: Identical. Same furniture. Same appliances. The view. Paul's even playing the same game as me. Pretty violent for a kid. He switches guns. Assault rifle. Kicks open a door. Takes out some guys. Makes his way along a grey corridor. In the basement. Concrete bunker. Grey corridor. Kicking down doors, taking out guys. He's running through the compound. Shooting. Running.

19

Living room.

DEREK: I went running along the shore. This park. Old people. In track-suits. Moving slowly. In unison. Felt like I was part of something.

MADDIE: Daddy. When're you coming home?

DEREK: Soon.

MADDIE: Do you want to see the routine? I've been practising.

DEREK: Not now darling. Work.

MADDIE: Is the weather nice there? How's the weather?

DEREK: Hot. When people come into the service station, they're hot and sweaty. Even at night. Sticky. Inside, it's air-conditioned so I'm just sitting around freezing. Sometimes I go out by the pumps to warm up. Been helping Gloria with her lines?

MADDIE: Yep.

DEREK: Good girl.

Silence.

You would have loved it. All these old people in tracksuits moving in slow-motion.

GLORIA: I'm uncomfortable with the material.

DEREK: Synchronicity.

GLORIA: In my dreams, I'm her.

DEREK: Could have run forever. Under the palms. It's so frigging clean. You go to jail for spitting or sticking your gum under a bench.

GLORIA: I wake up tired. Like I spent the whole night underground. Can't face rehearsals.

DEREK: You'll be fine.

GLORIA: Just want to stay up here. Safe.

DEREK: Get Maddie to help with your lines. You're good at this.

GLORIA: An old man on the bus stared at me.

DEREK: He what?

GLORIA: Stared.

DEREK: Well he probably recognised you.

GLORIA: His eyes. Stripped me. His wrinkly body. Hot and sticky. Derek? Are you there? The connection's really. You're frozen.

20

The balcony.

CLIENT: What a view.
CASSIE: Yes.
CLIENT: Wow.
CASSIE: The lights. Boats.
CLIENT: That building there. See?
CASSIE: With the palm on the roof?
CLIENT: Yeah. They got a pool up there.

Pause.

I'm on the tenth floor. View's nothing like this. This is wow.
CASSIE: Can I get you a drink?
CLIENT: A drink. Yeah nice. Thank you.

21

Living room.

DEREK: Am I still frozen? I'm moving my arms. Am I still frozen? Shit. Gloria? You're breaking up. All pixelated. Sweetheart? Now you're frozen. Shit.

22

Bathroom.

CASSIE *splashes water on her face.*

CASSIE: I'm melting. Jesus. My last one was scary. Short bald guy. Stank of cigarettes. Asked if he had to wear a condom. About half the men ask. I put it on him. Spun me round. Hard. Against the mirror. I wasn't expecting it. I was really fucking scared. Never know. Which guy might end up being unsafe.

Puts on lipstick.

Put my face on. Get back out there.

23

Living room.

PAUL: Do you know where my mum is?
JARED: She went out.
PAUL: With one of her friends?
JARED: I don't know where she.
PAUL: Are you and my mum friends?
JARED: I don't really know her.
PAUL: Do you want to be her friend?

Silence.

CASSIE: Make yourself comfortable.
CLIENT: I will thanks.
JARED: I only just met her.
PAUL: How come you're here?
JARED: I'm looking after you. I'm a neighbour.
PAUL: I don't know you.
CLIENT: I feel like we. Even though we only. Like I know you.
CASSIE: We've only just met.
CLIENT: This thing between us.
PAUL: How much is she paying you?
CLIENT: A bond.
JARED: Just. Normal rates.
CLIENT: Anything I'm not allowed to do?
CASSIE: Stay respectful and we'll be fine.
CLIENT: Can we kiss?
CASSIE: Yes you can kiss me.
CLIENT: I can? Really?
CASSIE: Sure. Go ahead.
CLIENT: Wow so it's not true that stuff in movies how the guy's in love with a working girl but she won't let him kiss her because she's saving her kisses for a man she hasn't even met yet but loves with every fibre of her being until *finally* she realises *oh shit wow* it's actually him after all—he's *the one*—the one she's been saving her kisses for, and when they finally kiss, wow it's the moment we've all been waiting

for, after all the confusion, they found each other and it's absolute fucking magic.

CASSIE: You can kiss me. Really it's fine.

They kiss.

JARED: Dead. Got shot. We watch in replay. A bullet hits him in the shoulder and jerks his body back. Next enters his skull. Blood sprays in the fluorescent air of the concrete bunker. He twirls slo-mo. Blood cloud billows. Dead.

DEREK: Fuck.

CASSIE: I do it for him.

CLIENT: I want to be your.

CASSIE: I want him to have a future.

GLORIA: I can't breathe.

DEREK: Fuck it.

CLIENT: Friends. Can we be friends?

PAUL: Wanna play?

JARED: No thanks. I'm fine.

CLIENT: Is everything okay? You seem a bit.

DEREK: I'm frozen. Fuck.

CASSIE: I'm fine.

CLIENT: Are you upset?

GLORIA: Help me. I can't.

CASSIE: No. No. I'm fine.

CLIENT: Aren't you enjoying?

CASSIE: I'm fine. It's good. Feels good.

DEREK: Fuck, fuck, fuck.

PAUL: You seem.

CLIENT: Not really here.

PAUL: Just sitting there.

CLIENT: Am I boring you?

PAUL: Can have a go. If you want.

CASSIE: I'm fine. Really.

JARED: I'm fine.

DEREK: Am I still frozen?

GLORIA: Help me please.

PAUL: Wanna play a game?

JARED: Said I'm fine.

PAUL: No I mean like a real game.

DEREK: My arms and legs are numb. Face numb. Frozen.

MADDIE *twirls her ribbons.*

Can't move. Stuck. Can't feel my face.

GLORIA: Are you listening?

CASSIE: I don't feel a thing.

PAUL: You count. I'll hide.

DEREK: Beautiful darling. Wow, getting good. Really coming along.

JARED: Ten nine eight seven six—

CLIENT: TV flickers. Mute. Can't believe she left it on. During.

JARED: Coming ready or not.

CLIENT: War. Concrete.

MADDIE: Been practising.

CLIENT: Dust and blood.

JARED: Coming to get you.

GLORIA: I don't know. If now's the right time. For.

CASSIE: He paid. Do what he wants.

DEREK: Please.

GLORIA: For us to. Me. I.

MADDIE: Want to go in a competition, feel that. Everyone cheering when you pull off a move.

CASSIE: It doesn't *mean* anything. It's a transaction.

DEREK: We *need*. For us.

CASSIE: Fake it.

GLORIA: If I can.

CLIENT: Chopper strafing. Slo-mo. Miniature people. Falling.

GLORIA: Into the world.

DEREK: Please darling. Us.

GLORIA: Right now.

MADDIE: Can I Daddy? Please.

CLIENT: Pixels.

GLORIA: When are you coming home?

CASSIE: I do it for him. My son.

JARED: Paul. Paul.

Silence.

Okay Paul, you win. You can come out now.

Silence.

I looked everywhere.

CASSIE: What do you mean everywhere?

JARED: Gone. I can't find.

CASSIE: People don't. PAUL.

JARED: I looked everywhere. He's not.

CASSIE: He can't just disappear. People don't just.

MADDIE: I want the whole world looking at me twirling, spinning, leaping. I want them to roar with happiness.

CASSIE: He can't.

GLORIA: If I can.

MADDIE: Daddy.

GLORIA: Handle this.

DEREK: We're not allowed to leave the hotel.

GLORIA: With everything.

MADDIE: Where's Daddy?

GLORIA: Mexico.

DEREK: I'm in Mexico City, sweetheart. We're not allowed to leave the hotel. The insurance doesn't cover us if we're out in the city unprotected. Every morning we get escorted from the lobby by security and driven in shiny black vans to meetings in tall glass buildings in this area with other glass buildings where we teach protocols and installation procedures. We step them through the training materials, get the system running, then security bundles us in the vans, back to the hotel, safely inside in the lobby.

MADDIE: When's he coming?

GLORIA: Soon darling.

CASSIE: He can't just disappear.

JARED: He hid.

CASSIE: Hid?

JARED: He was hiding.

CASSIE: From you? Hiding from you?

DEREK: We kill time around the pool. Or watch Mexican soap operas in our rooms.

JARED: Yeah.

CASSIE: Why would he do that Jared? Why would a little boy want to hide from you?

MADDIE: Why doesn't he come home?

DEREK: I feel at home in the hotel. Anonymous. Flipping channels.

CASSIE: You're sick. You know that? Sick.

GLORIA: I'm freezing. Darling shut the door.

CASSIE: PAUL. PAUL. PAUL.

Silence.

CLIENT: Is she even paying attention?

Silence.

I'm paying. I can do what I want.

CASSIE: I spoke to security. There's nothing on the surveillance. They checked the hallway. The entire floor. Elevators. Nothing. We looked everywhere. I told them. They said no way he left the apartment. They know—can see—who comes and goes. He's not on tonight's footage. They said he must still be in here. But we've looked and looked. Jesus. PAUL? PAUL? DARLING. YOU CAN COME OUT NOW. MUMMY'S HERE. MUMMY'S HOME. PLEASE, BABY.

JARED: I was in the corner. Watching. I wasn't supposed to be there. They didn't want me there. She held a knife to his throat and with one clean slice, she cut his throat. Like this—

He demonstrates.

CASSIE: You fuck. You sick fuck.

CLIENT: Hey, calm.

JARED: Don't. Please don't.

CASSIE: How dare you.

CLIENT: Calm down.

JARED: Calm.

MADDIE: Where are you?

CASSIE: Do you have any idea what you've.

DEREK: I watch porn. Drink beer from the minibar.

CASSIE: How dare.

GLORIA: They want me to go back.

MADDIE: Come home.

DEREK: What?

GLORIA: They want me to go. Visit. The rooms where.

DEREK: Do you think that's a good?

JARED: With one clean. A slice. His little neck.

GLORIA: Where it happened. The cellar.

JARED: He drops into her arms. She lowers his body. Closes his eyes. Kisses his eyes.

CASSIE: [*weeping*] Come back. Please come back. Darling, come back.

DEREK: Do you think that's a good.

GLORIA: My life.

JARED: She cradles him. He actually looks like me. Doesn't move.

MADDIE: The ribbons.

CLIENT: Afterwards. I feel sick.

GLORIA: I want this.

MADDIE: Twirling.

CLIENT: The forty or so seconds of the orgasm is the only bit that's any good. The rest—withdrawing money from the machine, the chitchat, pumping someone who couldn't care less—makes me want to disappear. Afterwards I just drive. Empty streets. The smell of her.

MADDIE: Falling. Twirling.

CASSIE: Please.

GLORIA: Home.

24

Gloria's bedroom.

DEREK: Her hair's damp. Her nightgown clings to her skin. The house is quiet. Her breathing.

Silence.

My wife.

25

Living room.

JARED: When did you get?

DEREK: It's corrective. My overbite.

JARED: Do you have any idea.

GLORIA: Jared. Leave him.
JARED: How frigging ridiculous you look, Derek?
DEREK: I got the clear ones. Ceramic. So they blend in.
JARED: Can't even talk properly.
MADDIE: How long do you have to wear them for?
DEREK: Two, two and a half years.
JARED: Have you heard yourself?
MADDIE: What are they for?
DEREK: They'll align and straighten Daddy's teeth. For dental health.
JARED: Brace face.
DEREK: It's—a good step.
GLORIA: Jared. Grow up.
JARED: Metal mouth.
DEREK: Ceramic actually. They're ceramic.
MADDIE: Will I have to have braces?
GLORIA: I don't think so darling.
DEREK: These are from Mexico.

He gives presents to MADDIE *and* JARED. *Sombreros.*

A rather long silence.

It's good for my career. Help me go places.
GLORIA: You're away all the time.
DEREK: I mean.
GLORIA: I know.
DEREK: Don't you want to kiss me?

They kiss.

Do they get in the way?
GLORIA: It's fine. I'll get used to it.
DEREK: Have you been thinking about?
GLORIA: Yes and I want to.
DEREK: Really? I thought you—really?
GLORIA: I think it'd be good for me.
DEREK: *Good for us*. I want this too.
GLORIA: I mean.
DEREK: Great, this is really great.
GLORIA: I'm talking about.
DEREK: Just what we need.

GLORIA: The show.

DEREK: Oh.

GLORIA: I meant the show.

Silence.

He flips channels on the television. Sound on mute. Cars on fire. You can hear the burning. Close. Down there. In the streets. Distorted. A slowed-down howl.

Silence.

They want me to visit where she was kept. The actual rooms.

Silence.

JARED: I place the shots where I like. The head. Or leg if I want them to fall first.

Silence.

GLORIA: Where he kept her. That pig. Rehearsals are tough. That fucking pig of a man. And Dominic. This tension. He knows I'm scared and he's pushing. Can't help himself. Like he wants to humiliate me. And well now there's this idea to visit the rooms. The actual cellar. Dominic thinks it might help. And the documentary. You know they're filming rehearsals right? There's a lot of interest in Dominic right now. In the project. In me. Anyway. They want to film me there. My reactions. Derek? Where he kept her. Her whole childhood. The monster.

DEREK: Can you believe this is happening? Can you believe this is happening here?

MADDIE: I stand on tippy toes and look down. Noise. Sirens. And this roar. Like an animal in pain. Things smashing. Burning.

DEREK: It's okay. We're safe up here. Jesus. Can you believe it?

GLORIA: Where's Jared?

MADDIE: He said to tell you he went out.

GLORIA: Fuck.

26

Living room.

JARED: How's Paul?

CASSIE: Fine. With his father. Custody.

JARED: Down there?
CASSIE: I spoke to them. He's fine.
JARED: Are you scared?
CASSIE: We're safe up here.

Pause.

You can smell the burning.
JARED: Do you ever get.
CASSIE: What?
JARED: Lonely. When Paul's not here.
CASSIE: I miss him of course. He's my boy.
JARED: Do you sleep with people—men—for money?

Pause.

CASSIE: Is that what?
JARED: I heard. Yes. That you.
CASSIE: I do it so.
JARED: Do you think we?
CASSIE: For his future. I'm sorry—what?

Pause.

JARED: I saved up. From the babysitting.
CASSIE: Jared, I don't think.
JARED: I'm scared. The riots.

Silence.

My first. Please. With you.

Silence.

CASSIE: You're a boy.
JARED: Can I kiss you?
CASSIE: Smoke. Noise.

Pause.

We're safe up here.
JARED: I have money.

27

Paul's room.

PAUL: I got lost. Went into a room. Mummy wasn't there. It wasn't our house but the stuff was the same. I called. She didn't come. No-one. The TV. No sound. Men and women dancing. In circles. Everybody clapped. No sound. I called for my mummy.

28

Living room.

GLORIA: Have you seen Jared?
MADDIE: No.
GLORIA: He's not in his room.
DEREK: He'll miss breakfast.
MADDIE: He hasn't slept at home for days.
GLORIA: What?
MADDIE: You didn't know?
GLORIA: Where is he?
MADDIE: Maybe he got a girlfriend. How would I know? Leave me alone.

29

Living room.

PAUL *comes in.*

CASSIE: You shouldn't be here darling.

Pause.

You should be in bed sweetheart.

Pause.

Jared is visiting Mummy. He came to say hi to Mummy.

Pause.

PAUL: I can't sleep. The noise.
CASSIE: We're safe up here.
PAUL: I had a bad dream.
CASSIE: I'll come tuck you in soon, sing you a song. Go to bed.

JARED: Paul. It's late. Go to bed.

JARED *kisses* CASSIE. *A deep kiss.* PAUL *just stares.*

30

Living room.

GLORIA: They want me to relive it.
DEREK: What?
GLORIA: The cellar. My reactions. So people.

Silence.

The documentary. I want to do it.

Silence.

They're offering good.
DEREK: This is not about.
GLORIA: It's *generous*. And Dominic.
DEREK: It's never been about the.
GLORIA: You could be here more.
DEREK: I'm.
GLORIA: You wouldn't have to go away so much.

Pause.

DEREK: If this is what you. If you think it's good.
GLORIA: The actual rooms. Where her father kept her.
DEREK: For you.

Silence.

Do you like my new teeth?

31

Cassie's room.

JARED: She's not porcelain. Her face isn't painted on. She's real. Like me. The noise from the streets doesn't wake her. She reaches for me in her sleep.

She does.

When I was a little, I used to watch my mother working. Rehearsals.

Sometimes they kicked me out. *Grown-up scenes*. But I snuck in. Watched from under a table or behind a piece of scenery. Once she was holding—cradling—this boy. He looked just like me. She held a kitchen knife to his neck.

He demonstrates.

And sliced. Clean. A slit. Now he was heavier. She lowered his body. Kissed his eyes. Calm. Full of love. Like a mother. I wanted to forget. I never forgot. She reaches in her sleep. From a dream. For me.

He strokes her face.

32

Living room.

MADDIE: I want to talk to Daddy.
GLORIA: The time sweetheart.
MADDIE: I need to talk to him.
GLORIA: Time difference.
MADDIE: I need to ask him something. Important.
GLORIA: Were you asleep?
DEREK: Is everything?
GLORIA: Maddie wants to.
MADDIE: Needs.
GLORIA: To ask you.
MADDIE: When Mummy died did you still love her? Do you still love her?
DEREK: I.

Silence.

MADDIE: Gloria says nothing. Sits and stares. Frozen. Sometimes hours. Or repeats. Like she'll be telling me something or asking me how my day was and she just repeats how was your day like she never even asked the first time. Like she totally forgot.
PAUL: Mummy. The noise. I can't sleep.
MADDIE: Her hands shake. She tries to hide it.
PAUL: Will they take our TV? Will they smash our things?
MADDIE: One night, I got up to go to the loo. She was dancing. Alone.

Holding her arms around herself. Like this—

She demonstrates.

Turning slowly. She didn't see me.

Silence. GLORIA *dances.* MADDIE *watches.*

DEREK: Is there anything you need? I can. There's this huge market here in an underground carpark. It's really bright. Handbags, shoes, sunglasses. You name it. The latest. And cheap. Gloria?

GLORIA: Music. Far away.

She dances.

DEREK: Gloria? Jesus. Thin air.

MADDIE: Daddy are you there?

DEREK *dances with* GLORIA. *A slow shuffle.*

GLORIA: Daddy.

Dancing.

PAUL: The noise.

JARED: Want to play a game?

PAUL: Mummy.

CASSIE: The view.

JARED: Yes.

CASSIE: Can see forever.

JARED: Yes. I kiss her neck. Soft.

Pause.

I want to join the fighting. Protect us. A soldier.

CASSIE: Jared. You.

Pause.

It's still burning.

33

Living room.

DEREK: Where is everybody? MADDIE. MADDIE. Where's Maddie?

GLORIA: Why are you?

DEREK: Where is she?

GLORIA: Shouting.

DEREK: I looked in her room. Everywhere. Her ribbons. The balcony.

GLORIA: Stop shouting all the.

DEREK: I'M NOT SHOUTING. WHERE'S MADDIE? WHERE THE FUCK IS SHE?

GLORIA: Since when?

DEREK: WHERE?

GLORIA: When did you start being so?

DEREK: I'M LOUD OKAY AT THE FOOTBALL AT THE BAR CRACKING JOKES MY MATES LOUD FUCKING LOUD I'M A LOUD FUCKER. NOW WHERE'S MY DAUGHTER?

GLORIA: We were watching TV. Dancing.

DEREK: ARE YOU DRUNK? JESUS. CAN'T LEAVE YOU ALONE. MADDIE. MADDIE.

GLORIA: A family again.

DEREK: Jesus. I can't.

GLORIA: Dominic yells at me. Now you. You never used.

DEREK: Jesus. The noise.

GLORIA: He doesn't believe in me. The role. But. At night. Down there. Cold. The walls. And music. The river. Muck. Those rooms.

34

Street.

MADDIE: I heard the noise, saw the fires. The burning smell. And on TV. Windows smashed. People carrying stuff. Police. I stood on the balcony and didn't have that feeling I might jump. I wasn't afraid. We weren't allowed to go down but I wanted to see for myself. Security was protecting our building. Standing around. Watching their monitors. Didn't stop me. Like I was invisible. On TV they said that the looters were criminals. Animals. I wanted to see.

35

The walls close in.

GLORIA: Is anyone there? Somebody. Please.

Silence.

Can you hear me? Please. Someone.

Silence.

Please. Please.

Silence.

Listen.

Silence.

The river.

Fade.

▼ ▼ ▼ ▼ ▼

TWO

A room without windows.

GLORIA *alone.*

GLORIA: Back?

Pause.

Coming back here?

Pause.

Give me a moment.

Silence.

Okay.

Pause.

Coming back? How I feel coming here? It's—

A GIRL *of around twelve enters and stands beside* GLORIA. *She might be the young* GLORIA.

A long silence.

GIRL: You—you grew.
GLORIA: Yes. I'm grown-up now.

Silence.

GIRL: Do you still think about me?
GLORIA: Yes.

Pause.

Of course I do. Yes.
GIRL: Remember when we saw the sky? Huge and white. Remember?
GLORIA: It hurt my eyes.
GIRL: Yes. Can you hear the river?
GLORIA: No.
GIRL: Daddy says the river is ancient.

The GIRL *has a doll. A baby. She makes it crawl around the room.*

Mummy's little girl. We call her Maddie. Daddy and me. Hello Maddie.

GLORIA: Shhh.

GIRL: I feed her.

GLORIA: I don't want to.

Footsteps are heard on the ceiling.

GIRL: Daddy.

Silence. They listen. After a while a MAN *enters. Sits. Reads a newspaper.*

GLORIA: Do you know who I am?

Silence.

Don't you recognise?

Silence.

MAN: [*to the* GIRL] What was that? Did you say something darling?

GIRL: How was your day?

MAN: Fine. Just fine.

GIRL: Did you walk along the river?

MAN: Not today darling. I was busy. All day.

GLORIA: No.

GIRL: Did you bring me something?

MAN: Like what?

GLORIA: I shouldn't be here.

GIRL: Something special.

GLORIA: I can't.

GIRL: A present.

GLORIA: I'm freezing.

GIRL: The river.

MAN: You can't have presents every day.

GIRL: I know.

GLORIA: I'm sorry.

MAN: But since you were such a good girl looking after Maddie.

GIRL: Daddy!

He produces a small package wrapped in tissue paper and gives it to her.

GLORIA: The bird.

The GIRL *opens it. A painted tin bird.*

MAN: Do you?

GLORIA: It's beautiful. Thank you.

MAN: You squeeze the handle. The wings. To make it fly.

The GIRL *does.*

Like that.

GIRL: Thank you. I love it.

MAN: How's Maddie?

GIRL: She's good. We were—

GLORIA: Playing.

The MAN *picks up the doll and plays with her, lifting her in the air above him, smiling and making faces.*

MAN: [*to the doll*] Hello little one. Say hello. My precious little girl. Hello Maddie.

GIRL: There's a house on top of ours. They had a little girl but she died. Now they're sad.

GLORIA: Why?

GIRL: She went out. It wasn't safe. She got lost.

MAN: What about you?

GIRL: I'm happy here, Daddy.

GLORIA: Where's Dominic? [*Screams.*] Dominic!

She hides her face and sobs. The GIRL *is distressed.*

Where's fucking Dominic?

MAN: Why don't you go to your room darling? Take Maddie, read her a story.

The GIRL *leaves with the doll.*

Can't you see you're upsetting her, Gloria.

Pause.

Gloria?

GLORIA *sobs.*

Calm.

MAN: Jesus Gloria. You stink of booze.

GLORIA: I'm—

MAN: Fuck's sake.

GLORIA: What? What?

MAN: Get a grip.

GLORIA: I'm fine.

MAN: I believe in you. Dominic does too. What you're doing here is brave.

GLORIA: I feel fake. Air. A window. Jesus.

MAN: What's there to see?

GLORIA: What if she?

MAN: What?

GLORIA: Wants to see.

MAN: See what? You have no idea.

GLORIA: The world.

MAN: Do you have any idea how dangerous it is out there. Drugs. Scum. Men who want to hurt her. She's safe here. We're a family. Happy.

The GIRL *enters.*

She practises with her ribbon.

Hey that's coming along.

GIRL: Been practising.

MAN: Good.

She practises. He watches.

GIRL: Is she okay?

MAN: All better now.

GIRL: All better.

Silence.

You like it?

GLORIA: What?

The GIRL *shows her the ribbon.*

GIRL: My ribbon. Daddy gave it to me. I'm learning a routine.

GLORIA: I remember.

GIRL: Daddy gave it me.

She twirls the ribbon.

GLORIA: You're getting good. [*Correcting*] Gave me it.

GIRL: You have to keep the ribbons moving. Not allowed to stop. This is *twirl* and this is *spiral* and this one *snake* and *loop-the-loop.* Look—*flowers.*

She performs her routine. The MAN*'s phone rings. He leaves. Sound of a door being locked. Sound of someone moving upstairs. Then silence, the ribbons.*

GLORIA: You don't have to do that. With the ribbons. Just to please him.

The GIRL *slows the ribbons down.*

You don't have to believe his stories. It's stuff he makes up. To keep you here.

The GIRL *stops and listens, ribbons hanging, head bowed.*

The world isn't a prison. It's glorious. And you're part of it.

The sound of something being dragged upstairs.

The river isn't polluted. It's not filled with muck and animals. It's a normal brown river flowing from the mountains to the sea. Through our city where it's broad and gentle. The people who founded our city decided this was a good place to live. Fresh water for drinking, washing clothes, swimming. Fishing, boats, trade. You should see the river on a summer afternoon. It's glorious. Like everything might dissolve. Or on foggy mornings when people crossing bridges are ghosts. Or night. Alone. The lights. Rippling.

The GIRL *trembles with fear or excitement.*

The sky is vast. It hangs. Like a sheet. Eye. Egg. You feel it. Humming. You stand on a bridge and watch the water transporting memories and dreams. You feel small. Part of a gigantic world.

Sound of faraway music. The MAN *returns.*

[*To the* MAN] Do you remember me?

Silence. The music. The MAN *ignores her.*

Don't you recognise me?

Silence. The music. The GIRL *crosses to the* MAN *and takes his hand.*

I remember.

The MAN *and the* GIRL *dance a slow waltz.* GLORIA *watches. They dance like this until the music stops. The* GIRL *holds the* MAN. *He doesn't move. Something wooden and stiff about how he stands. Like a marionette.*

GIRL: I want to go outside.

Silence. The GIRL *hugging the* MAN.

MAN: It's not safe.
GIRL: Maddie wants to see the river.
MAN: How do you know?
GIRL: She told me.
MAN: She can't talk.
GIRL: She wants to walk in the sun.
MAN: The river's dirty.
GIRL: It's not, it's not.
MAN: Foul. Baby carriage, dead horse, bloated. Filth.
GIRL: No.

Silence. The GIRL *trembles.*

MAN: What about Maddie?

The GIRL *looks at the doll.*

Let me go.

She lets him go.

Doll.

She picks up the doll.

Wall.

She walks to the wall.

Face.

She faces the wall.

We're lucky. We don't need anyone.

GLORIA *spits in the* MAN*'s face. He doesn't react, doesn't wipe it away.*

GIRL: [*still facing wall*] Lucky.
MAN: Perfect life.

GIRL: Perfect.

MAN: No-one will ever harm you.

GLORIA: Disgusting. Pig. Animal. I hate you.

She attacks the MAN, *hits him, claws at him, but he doesn't react.*

Sick sick pig. You sick fucking pig.

GIRL: [*still facing wall*] Leave Daddy alone. Stop it. You're hurting him.

GLORIA: You monster.

GLORIA *attacks him. He's completely impassive. Slowly, with a minimum of effort, he gains control and holds her until she exhausts herself. The* GIRL *stands against the wall. The doll hanging from her hand.*

Let me go.

He releases her.

I'm. I can't. I'm sorry—

GLORIA *leaves the room. Silence. The* GIRL *relaxes, i.e. stops facing the wall.*

MAN: You okay darling?

GIRL: I'm okay.

MAN: It's a tough scene. I know.

GIRL: I'm okay. What're we doing now?

MAN: I think we're taking some kind of a break.

GIRL: Is she okay?

MAN: She'll be fine. She's all wound up. The role.

The MAN*'s phone rings.*

Just a second, darling.

He answers it as he leaves. The GIRL *is left alone. She plays with the doll.*

GIRL: It's okay. Mummy's here.

Another MAN, *wearing an earpiece enters, whispers to the* GIRL. *They leave together. She leaves the doll lying on the floor. After some time, another* WOMAN *enters. Dressed like* GLORIA.

WOMAN: By myself yes no intimacy prefer alone yes of course I think about him every day mostly gentle kind sometimes funny yes he told me stories presents great with the children a real joker great dad of course I cried when I heard he was dead I have a heart knew they were hunting him panicked strange in front of a train I always imagined him drowning in that filthy river bloated shame yes I fantasised about killing him sawing his head off you saw where I lived on TV right cold damp disgusting no windows fluoro light preserved alive Nerfertiti stuck awake wondering what happens if he dies I die nobody knows and my children what about them sometimes yes he let me upstairs curtains always drawn booby-trapped he said we lived a normal life I cooked cleaned watched TV looked after the babies we didn't need anyone he said no-one to harm me yes sent back under when visitors came he wiped every surface not just to hide traces of me he was obsessed order cleanliness bind my hair with clips wear the plastic shower cap to catch stray hairs shave myself bald saying for hygiene not allowed to cry never because salt traces DNA then he choked me head under water for example fingerprint on glass once I stole a look through the curtains sky bright so bright then yes the end the garage on knees cleaning car his phone rang because the vacuuming was loud off he walked took my chance jumped gate ran ran ran climbing fences calling help police please no-one stopped only that one lady brought me in the police the medical I said save my children please on television they said the children were speaking a made-up language like animals I remember flashes cameras outside the station yes I read the headlines victim stamped on my head no I almost never go out my favourite activity is reading plus breeding cacti taking photos I prefer inside glasses on a table a few leaves from the philodendron over there—

She points. There is no pot plant.

The way light falls in a room, details.

She leaves the room. The room is empty. Distant music. At last, the GIRL *enters and plays with the doll. The* MAN *comes in and sits, watches her play.* GLORIA *enters dressed in her underwear. Eyes red from crying. Or glycerine.* MAN 2, *wearing the earpiece, follows her in, stands in corner.*

MAN 2: Good. Okay.

GLORIA *sits.*

A few close-ups.

GLORIA: Sitting or?

MAN 2: That's good.

He listens to the earpiece.

Okay Gloria. He wants to hear the new text. The *shattered speech*. Her interior.

She just stares.

Gloria?

GLORIA: Okay.

MAN 2: Remember what he said? You heard him. He believes in you.

GLORIA: Yes.

MAN 2: Her story. The shattered.

MAN 2 *withdraws.*

GLORIA: Yes.

Long silence.

Think flesh sky yes blood ribbon bird.

She sits with eyes closed.

Open clean help.

The GIRL *leaves the doll and picks up the tin bird.*

Crawl wall music baby spit cold river white.

MAN: Good.

GLORIA: Face hole sky.

The GIRL *makes the tin bird fly.*

MAN: Good. That's good. Do it again.

Will she? Fade.

▼ ▼ ▼ ▼ ▼

THREE

Theatre dressing-room.

DEREK: Do you like my teeth?
JARED: What?
DEREK: My new teeth.
JARED: Nice. Must've cost.
DEREK: You know.
JARED: Cosmetic.
DEREK: Corrective.
JARED: Oh. Right.
DEREK: Do you like them?
JARED: Derek. They're not exactly new.
DEREK: I know but I'm asking if.
JARED: Brace face.
DEREK: Okay.
JARED: Metal mouth.
DEREK: Porcelain.
JARED: Whatever.
DEREK: Porcelain and plastic.
JARED: Whatevs.
DEREK: Blends in.
JARED: Does it?
DEREK: My wife likes them.
JARED: [*sarcastic*] Your wife.
DEREK: Anyway. My bite needed correcting.
JARED: Ever get food stuck?
DEREK: Food what?
JARED: In between.
DEREK: What? No. Sometimes.
JARED: I met this girl in the bar. After-show last night. Ohmyfuckinggod.
DEREK: Hot?
JARED: What?
DEREK: Hot, was she hot?

JARED: Yes she was hot.

DEREK: And?

JARED: And what nothing. She dug the show. Thought it was edgy.

DEREK: Did she like my work?

JARED: She didn't really mention you.

DEREK: Okay.

JARED: Not specifically.

DEREK: But she liked the show?

JARED: She did.

DEREK: Great. That's great.

JARED: Actually, she liked your teeth.

DEREK: What?

JARED: Yeah. She loved them. Your metal smile.

DEREK: Porcelain. Did she?

JARED: No, no she didn't.

DEREK: Right.

JARED: She asked me to sign her program, blinking her fuck-me eyes.

DEREK: No way.

JARED: Yes way. She eye-fucked me.

He demonstrates.

DEREK: Jesus wept.

JARED: Yup.

DEREK: And?

JARED: And—weirdest thing—when she was sucking my dick she kept saying your name.

DEREK: She what?

JARED: Over and over. 'Derek, Derek.' Looking up. Mouth full. 'Derek. You're magnificent.'

DEREK: What? She didn't?

JARED: No she did not.

DEREK: Right.

JARED: [*pretending to have a full mouth*] 'Derek … oh, Derek … your teeth are perfect.'

DEREK: Ha-dee-fucking-ha.

JARED: Apparently Gloria doesn't want to go on.

DEREK: When does she?

JARED: She's in a foul mood.

DEREK: When is she not?

JARED: Is it true you and she once?

DEREK: What? Who?

JARED: Gloria. I heard.

DEREK: Well.

Slight pause.

JARED: Naughty naughty Derek.

DEREK: Once. A long time ago.

JARED: Dirty dog.

DEREK: We've been friends since drama school.

JARED: And?

DEREK: She's like a sister.

JARED: Oh you sick puppy.

DEREK: Not like that. Jesus.

JARED: And?

DEREK: What?

JARED: So?

DEREK: So what?

JARED: Did you bang her brains out?

DEREK: We were both pretty drunk.

JARED: I bet she was wild back then.

DEREK: I don't.

JARED: A stone-cold fox.

DEREK: She's.

JARED: And? Now? Would you go there?

DEREK: I don't know, she's.

JARED: Pretty fucking crazy, right.

DEREK: Having a rough time.

JARED: She's fucking mental, right?

DEREK: Jared.

JARED: And drunk. Always drunk. Man.

DEREK: Don't talk about her like.

JARED: She used to be so amazing. Incredible. I'd do her though.

DEREK: What?

JARED: Even though she's old.

DEREK: Whoa hang on she's hardly *old*.

JARED: C'mon, she's a total fucking MILF.

DEREK: Christ.

JARED: Pretty fucking wild. Am I right? Take me there Derek. Blow by blow.

DEREK: I'm not.

JARED: Wide-screen, slow-mo, uncut. Please Uncle Derek.

DEREK: Grow up.

JARED: She's still got a banging body.

DEREK: And?

JARED: She's got the hots for me is what.

DEREK: Right.

JARED: What?

DEREK: I said right as in uh-huh my friend don't think so.

JARED: Are you a teeny bit jealous Derek?

DEREK: As if.

JARED: I've seen how she looks at me.

MADDIE *enters.*

DEREK: Jesus. You actually believe that every man, woman and child.

JARED: Um.

DEREK: Wants to jump your skinny bones and fuck your silly brains out.

JARED: Derek.

DEREK: What?

JARED: Um.

DEREK: What you big stud?

He sings something sexy. Makes sexy moves in JARED*'s face.*

JARED: Maddie.

DEREK *sees* MADDIE.

DEREK: Oh. Hi.

MADDIE: Hi Derek.

DEREK: Did she?

JARED: Yep.

DEREK: Fuck.

MADDIE: Swear jar.

DEREK: Double fuck.

MADDIE: Pay up Daddy-O. Four bucks.

DEREK: Four? I only said three fucks.
MADDIE: Okay now it's five. The F-word thrice plus the double F-word.
DEREK: Jesus.

He pays her.

You been warming up Maddie?
MADDIE: Yeah, you should try it sometime. Might help.
JARED: Did you see Gloria out there?
MADDIE: In the corridor. She's said she's not going on.
DEREK: She what?
MADDIE: Kip's talking to her. She's drunk.
DEREK: Maddie.
MADDIE: She can't even stand up properly. Plus she refuses to wear her wig. Kip says she has to. She says no f-ing way and now she's not going on. He tells her she looks amazing in it. That the wig—actually, he says *hairpiece*—is a key to her character. She tells him to go f-ing f-himself. Kip's trying to stay calm but you can tell he's totally stressed. He turned scarlet. Have we had the half?
DEREK: Yep.

MADDIE *does her vocal warm-up. Stretches etc.*

JARED: Do you like Derek's new teeth?
MADDIE: Yeah sure they're fine.
DEREK: Thanks sweetheart.
JARED: Had an audition today.
DEREK: What for?
JARED: This 3D apocalypse thing, it's bullshit.
MADDIE: Kerching.

MADDIE *puts her hand out.* JARED *pays her.*

JARED: Wait.

He gives her another dollar.

Seriously, it's *fucking* stupid. The Earth's been completely destroyed and New York's a—

He gives her another dollar.

Total fucking wasteland. Lawless. Gangs, mutants, terror. Fucking mayhem.

She puts out her hand.

Wait. Anyway, I'm part of this unit that's gone AWOL because we don't believe in the corruption and overall bad decision-making that has basically become fucking rampant in the what's left of the armed forces. We want to put things right, get ourselves out of this God-awful fucking shithole and make our way to California where there's still hope.

DEREK: Sorry what?

JARED: Hope. I said hope.

DEREK: What do you mean by hope?

JARED: Well, California is kinda okay, I mean compared to New York City, it's fucking paradise.

She puts out her hand.

I said wait, kiddo. People in Cali are on top of things, there's no chaos, sickness, mutants. In fact there's this big fuck-off fence separating the Free State of California from the rest of the US. There's me and the other guys in my unit plus this woman and kid and we're all trying to get to California. We're up to our necks in violence and desperation and mayhem—*the shit*—just trying to make it through each fucking day. To stay full of courage, free and alive. Anyway, the scene I did today, it's pretty bullshit. Some kind of flashback. I'm showering. Washing off blood. In a white-tiled room. These other guys are showering too. Soldiers. Guys my age plus old guys too. Maybe it's the start of the war, they didn't say. Anyway, my character is washing blood off. He's covered in gore. He sees the other guys through the steam scrubbing blood off their bodies too. It's like part of the daily routine. But it's as if he's seeing it for the first time. He doesn't want to end up like the old guys. Doesn't want to be stuck here fighting this goddamn war for whatever fucking reason. The old guys are a premonition. The future he doesn't want to be part of. He wants out. That's fucking it. He's going AWOL. To California and freedom. How much?

MADDIE: Sixteen.

JARED: [*pays her*] Twenty and I want credit.

DEREK: And?

JARED: And what?

DEREK: How did you go?

JARED: Wasn't feeling it. And the director, I don't think he liked my choices.

DEREK: Damn bro.

JARED: Hey Maddie, there's a good role for you. This kid, this girl, she's like on the run disguised as a boy because it's safer for her like that. You should read for it.

MADDIE: My agent already discussed it with me. We don't think it's right for me. Anyway I don't want to do clichéd work. I only want to do work that's got integrity.

Pause.

What if she doesn't go on? Will they cancel?

DEREK: She'll go on.

MADDIE: All those people lining up to see her.

DEREK: Us. See us.

JARED: They want to see her fuck up. Forget her lines. Fall on her face. Total meltdown.

DEREK: Jared.

MADDIE: [*robot voice*] You have three swear credits remaining.

JARED: It's true. They love a catastrophe.

MADDIE: [*robot voice*] Top up now at wwwdotmaddierulesdotcom.

DEREK: You should cut her some slack.

JARED: She doesn't even *talk* to us anymore. You're supposed to be her old friend and when was the last time she even said boo to you? She's always pacing the corridors or outside chain-smoking, refusing to go on. And who knows what she'll say or do when she does go onstage? It's not the script. It's not what we agreed on. What would Dominic think?

DEREK: Dominic's not here.

JARED: Hey Maddie. Fuckity fuck her and her fucking *hairpiece.*

MADDIE: [*robot voice*] You have zero dollars credit and zero dollars my bonus swear credit.

JARED: I don't think he'd like it much. What she's doing. What she's turning his play into. She never listens to Kip.

DEREK: As if Kip can give her notes.

JARED: Kip's notes are good.

DEREK: They're fine. I like Kip don't get me wrong but c'mon she was never going to take notes from him. She barely listens to Dominic.
MADDIE: They call him the Sphinx.
DEREK: What? Who?
MADDIE: Kip. The Sphinx.
DEREK: Who does?
MADDIE: Alice and Dominic.
JARED: Why?
MADDIE: Because of how he sits there. So serious.
DEREK: How do you know?
MADDIE: Alice told me. I think it's meant to be a compliment.
DEREK: Does he know?
MADDIE: Uh-uh. No way.

MADDIE *goes out.*

JARED: I'm sick of her.
DEREK: Who? Maddie? Why?
JARED: What? No. Gloria.
DEREK: Right.
JARED: She makes it hard for me to go out there and be truthful.
DEREK: Look, sure it's been difficult lately.
JARED: She makes my blood freeze.

Pause.

DEREK: You should have seen her when she was young. Dangerous. My God. You never knew what she'd do next. Really incredible.
JARED: The one where she kills her son.
DEREK: Okay. Medea.
JARED: Was it? Anyway whatever. In-fucking-credible.
DEREK: You saw that?
JARED: The film.
DEREK: Right.
JARED: The way she held the knife. And his little body. Her eyes. So full of love. That shit blew my mind.

MADDIE *returns.*

She doesn't like them looking at her.
DEREK: Who?

JARED: The audience.

DEREK: What?

JARED: She actually says *why are they always staring at me*?

DEREK: It's some kind of breakdown.

JARED: Breakdown? She's a fucking train wreck.

MADDIE: Kerching.

He pays up.

Actually, do you guys mind keeping it down? I'm trying to get in the zone.

She goes out again.

DEREK: [*softly*] I never actually.

JARED: What?

DEREK: We never.

JARED: Whoa what are you saying?

DEREK: That night. We.

JARED: Hold on. What night?

DEREK: When we. She and I. Too drunk. Nervous or whatever.

JARED: But everyone.

DEREK: I know but it's not true.

JARED: Jesus Derek. Jesus fucking. You never?

DEREK: No.

JARED: Oh you poor fuck. You mean she. You're in bed with her and.

DEREK: Right. No.

JARED: Oh man. Derek. You were like my hero for about five minutes. I *idolised* you. Because back then she must have been the greatest fuck on earth. Oh Derek. No wonder deep down you're so fucking sad.

DEREK: She's a star, still a star, every inch a star.

JARED: She's mean and washed-up.

DEREK: You don't get it.

JARED: A shadow of her former.

DEREK: She's still got it.

JARED: Bullfuckingshit.

DEREK: They can't take their eyes off her. She's part of them. An embodiment of their innermost selves. However fucked-up she gets, however much the wheels fall off. Out there. Every night. Lining up for tickets. Because of her. We're nothing. She's burnt into their minds. Her Nina, her Hedda, her Gertrude, her Clytemnestra, her whoever. She puts it all out there. Her love, her rage, her longing, her selfishness, her ecstasy, her glory, her squalor, her sorrow, her ferocity.

JARED: Anything you've forgotten, Dirk?

DEREK: Her perversity, her *courage*, the child she once was, her great wit, every inch of her sexual being, her wounds, her scars, her endless fucking struggle not to collapse into the abyss.

Silence.

JARED: Nice.

DEREK: What?

JARED: Nice speech. No really. It was actually very moving.

DEREK: One day, you'll tell your grandchildren you worked with her.

JARED: [*laughs*] My what?

DEREK: That you were lucky enough to share a stage with her for a few hours of your pathetic, made-for-TV existence. You fluff.

JARED: Sorry, what did you just call me?

DEREK: Fluff. You piece of fluff.

JARED: Ouch Derek.

He feigns hurt. MADDIE *enters.*

MADDIE: Why's Jared crying?

JARED: [*through tears*] He called me fluff.

MADDIE: Jesus Derek. That's not very sensitive.

MADDIE *leaves again. She can't keep still. A bundle of nerves.*

DEREK: Washed-up. What would you know? Bred on video games and porn and bullshit 3D zombie.

JARED: Mutant.

DEREK: Mutant meaningless fucking junk and you think you have the right to pass judgement on her. On her performance.

MADDIE *returns. Loud vocal warm-up.*

Her career. Her *life*? What do you know? About life? About being an artist? Lightweight.

MADDIE: Who's lightweight?

DEREK: Jared.

JARED: Moi.

MADDIE: Whoa.

JARED: Fuck you Derek. I'm sick of you and your whole generation. Everything you did was so much better, so important. So *radical.* You did it all. And what's left for us? Crumbs. Endless copies. The facsimiles of your great invention. Well fuck you. You has-been.

MADDIE *laughs.*

Your world makes me sad. You're a pack of self-obsessed, stagnant, fake-as-fuck cunts.

MADDIE: Whoa.

JARED: Your world is dead and your precious fucking theatre is dead.

PAUL *wanders in and sits down. Listens.*

A pathetic fucking joke.

PAUL: What's a joke?

JARED: This. Theatre. Fakery. Lies.

PAUL: Oh.

Pause.

MADDIE: Don't say that. Jared. Please don't.

Pause.

I like it here. I like being with you guys. I like going onstage. Everyone watching. It makes me feel alive.

Silence.

By the way you owe the swear jar for five f-words and one c-word. Double for those uttered in reach of Paul's tender ears.

PAUL: Is it true we're not going on tonight? Will they send everyone away?

DEREK: We'll see mate.

JARED: A star. Burning out. Going going gone.

An announcement over the tannoy: 'Ladies and gentlemen, this is your five-minute call. You have five minutes until beginners.'

DEREK: Sounds like we're going on.

JARED: Does it?

Silence. KIP *enters.*

DEREK: Hey, it's The Kipper. Whaddup bro?

JARED: Hey Kipster.
MADDIE: Kip are we going on?
KIP: Sure thing, Maddie.
PAUL: Cool.

He wanders out.

JARED: Really?
KIP: Look we had a bit of a situation but it's sorted now so yeah.
MADDIE: Is she gonna wear the wig?
DEREK: Maddie.
KIP: Look I can't say.
DEREK: Got any notes for me?
KIP: What? Now?
DEREK: From last time?
KIP: You sure you want them now?
DEREK: It's okay. You in tonight dude?
KIP: Sure. Yep. Sure.
DEREK: Okay great. That's great. So notes?
KIP: Yep. Sure. Fine.
DEREK: Heard from Dominic? How is he?
KIP: Good. Having a good time.
JARED: Lucky guy.
DEREK: How about like a *general note*. Something overall to aim for tonight?
MADDIE: Guys please, a bit of shh around here.
DEREK: Sorry.

KIP*'s phone rings. An absurd ringtone.*

KIP: Hi, Dom … Yeah … I talked to her … Look maybe if you … Okay, fine … Yep, I'm with them now … Everyone, Dominic says hi.
ALL: Hi Dominic.
KIP: What sorry you're breaking up … He says he misses you and thinks about you every time you're doing a show … He calculates the time difference … Yeah I told them … Maddie's fine. Right?
MADDIE: Yep.
DEREK: Can I?
KIP: Sorry Derek, what?
DEREK: Can I have a quick word? Kip? With Dominic?

KIP: Really? … Okay be quick.

DEREK: Hi Dom … Sure man okay … [*Sings in a techno robot voice*] *'I'm bigger and badder and rougher and tougher, in other words sucker there is no other I'm the one and only Dominator …'* Yeah good man, good … How is it there?

Pause.

Right … Fuck … Wow … Sounds incredible.

He makes a 'sorry' face to MADDIE, *throws her a coin.*

Oh nothing really just wanted to ask if there was anything like advice, I'm feeling a bit you know stale and wanted to know if you had any special piece of advice, like a reminder or *key word,* you've been gone for ages and Kip's great but I'd really appreciate some—

Pause.

Right … Gotcha … Yeah, I can do that … Ha … Yeah why not … Thanks man … Yeah you too … Here's Kip …

He hands the phone back to KIP.

KIP: Yep yep okay …

He passes the phone to JARED.

JARED: Hey Dom.

Silence. JARED *listens. After some time, he passes the phone back to* KIP.

KIP: He's gone.

DEREK: What did he say?

JARED: Maddie block your ears.

MADDIE: What? Why?

JARED: Block them.

She does.

He said I should go out there and absolutely fucking destroy her.

Silence. DEREK *repeatedly opens and closes his mouth, part of his warm-up.* JARED *leaves the room.*

MADDIE: [*too loud*] Can I unblock my ears now?

DEREK: [*nods*] Yes sweetheart.

KIP: Have a good show guys.

DEREK: Thanks Kipster. Notes.

KIP: Later.

DEREK: Thanks bro.

MADDIE: 'Bye Kip.

Silence.

He's gone.

DEREK: The Sphinx. [*A funny voice*] The Riddle of the Sphinx.

He laughs too loud.

[*Again*] The Riddle of the Sphinx.

MADDIE: [*confused*] What?

DEREK: You know. The Sphinx.

MADDIE: What're you talking about?

DEREK: You know who The Sphinx is, right?

MADDIE: Sure. Kip.

DEREK: No. The actual Sphinx. Outside Thebes, beyond the gates, there's this statue in the desert. Huge. Face half gone. No-one remembers who carved it. Haunches of a lion, wings of a great bird, a woman's face. Anyone who wants to pass into Thebes has to answer her riddle or she strangles him and eats him.

MADDIE: Why do you say him?

DEREK: What?

MADDIE: Him. Why *him*? What if the traveller's a woman?

DEREK: Well in the story.

MADDIE: I bet I could answer the riddle. Bet The Sphinx would let me through.

GLORIA *enters.*

GLORIA: We're going on.

GLORIA *goes into another smaller room (her private dressing-room).*

MADDIE: [*a whisper*] Do you think she'll wear it?

DEREK: [*whisper*] What?

MADDIE: [*whisper*] The wig.

DEREK: [*whisper*] No idea.

Silence.

MADDIE: Derek?

DEREK: Yes sweetheart?

MADDIE: Can we run my lines? The speech where I run away.

DEREK: Okay. But quick. We don't have much time.

MADDIE: [*at a lick*] I didn't know if anyone was following me. I just ran. People everywhere. Carrying TVs. Bags of stuff. Smashing shop windows, burning cars. I wasn't scared. It was *wild.* The sky was huge.

DEREK: Vast.

MADDIE: The sky was vast. A milky eye. Watching me run. The city burned. I thought someone would stop me, ask where was I going but they didn't, not even the police. I'd never seen so many people. When I got to the river, it was on fire too. I stood on the bridge with everyone. Watching the river burn. I thought now anything is possible. A whole new life. How was that?

DEREK: Great. Spot-on. You know it.

MADDIE: Thanks.

Announcement: 'Ladies and gentleman, this is your beginners' call. This is your call to the stage.'

Here goes nothing.

DEREK: Have a good show.

MADDIE: Thanks you too.

They leave. Empty room. Silence. The hum of an audience is heard over the tannoy. After a while, GLORIA *emerges from her smaller, private room. She has the wig on. She checks herself in a mirror.*

GLORIA: Christ.

She leaves. Empty room. Audience hum. Nothing for a while. Then, MADDIE *runs back into the room. She forgot her ribbons. She picks them up from her dressing table. Takes a few deep breaths. Shakes her limbs. Stops. Looks in a mirror.*

MADDIE: You've got a dream, protect it. You want something, go get it.

MADDIE *runs out again. The empty dressing-room.* CASSIE *passes through. Stretching.*

CASSIE: [*quietly speed-running lines*] I put on my face. Sit at the mirror. Eyes. Lips. Colour my cheeks. I'm always like this. Before a date. You know. Butterflies. What type of man. What am I in for.

PAUL *enters.*

Let's go buster. High-five.

They high-five.

Alright.

They leave. The audience hum stops. Silence. Then JARED*'s voice can be heard on the tannoy.*

JARED'S VOICE: At night when I can't sleep, I walk through the rooms. Feet on the carpet. The refrigerator hums. Our house is a stage set and I'm the only living character. The others are puppets. Faces painted on.

GLORIA *enters. Under the following, strips and puts on a gold sequin dress.*

They lie in bed attached to strings. Snoring, mumbling, farting. Until the string jerks and up they get to play their parts.

GLORIA *stares at herself in a dressing-room mirror.*

Removes wig.

She laughs silently or is she crying?

She can't stop.

Fade.

▼▼▼▼▼

FOUR

1

Empty room.

JARED: I walk into this room I thought was empty. Routine check. I don't see her immediately. In a corner. Hands over head. Protecting. As if like that she'd be invisible. As if we might not see her and leave her alone. Like that. Trembling.

GLORIA, *wearing a torn gold sequin dress, in the corner. She looks the worse for wear.*

Dressed for a ball. Like a queen.

He helps her up.

This all happened years ago. I brought her home. Made her my wife.

She can hardly stand. He stops her from falling.

That's it. Try and stand. Gloria, stand up. That's it. Stay up. Good.

2

Living room.

CASSIE *is brushing* PAUL*'s hair.*

CASSIE: You look nice for when Mummy comes home.
PAUL: Ow.
CASSIE: Nearly done. Good.

She finishes. He sits on the sofa. She brings him a glass of milk. He drinks.

You've got a milk moustache.

She laughs. He wipes his mouth with his sleeve. Sound of door being opened.

That must be.
PAUL: Mummy.

JARED enters, carrying shopping bags.

JARED: Is she?
CASSIE: Not yet.
JARED: Been a good boy for Cassie? Did he behave?
CASSIE: An angel.
JARED: A present. For her premiere.

He shows her a dress.

CASSIE: Wow. It's.

Pause.

JARED: Why don't you.
CASSIE: She'll be back any.
JARED: Try.

She tries the dress on. He helps her with the zipper.

And the shoes.

He takes a pair of heels from a shopping bag.

CASSIE: I.

She puts them on.

JARED: Wow.

She walks around, a bit wobbly in the shoes. Looks at herself in a mirror.

You look absolutely.
CASSIE: I should really take it off.
JARED: Fucking amazing.

He stands behind her and kisses her neck. They look at themselves in the mirror. PAUL is watching.

3

Living room.

JARED *folds the dress, puts it and the shoes back in the bags.*

JARED: [*to* PAUL] Where's Mummy?

Pause.

Where's she got to?

Pause.

How about the zoo this weekend? With Dad? Check out the bird show?

Pause.

It's incredible. Man, the hawks. You should see. And these wedge-tailed eagles which swoop right over you. Whoosh. This huge eagle. Pick you up with his talons and whoosh.

Pretending to be an eagle, JARED *picks* PAUL *up and flies him around. Puts him down.* PAUL *straightens his hair, makes himself neat.*

What's up champ? You're quiet. Mum'll be home soon.

PAUL: I want to tell her.

JARED: Tell her what mate?

PAUL: About today. What happened.

JARED: Don't think that's a good.

PAUL: With Cassie.

Silence.

It was fun.

JARED: What?

PAUL: With Cassie. We made a cubby. She put spooky music on and we hid.

JARED: You won't say anything, will you? To Mummy.

PAUL: I want to go to the bird show. I want to see the eagle. Swooping.

JARED: We will mate. You and me. Daddy's gonna take a shower now. Okay?

PAUL: Yep.

4

Bathroom.

JARED *in shower.*

JARED: At work. The showers. White-tiled room. Dirty work. Steam. Blood. Hair, nails. Pink on the tiles. When will it be over? Old guys, naked and wrinkled in the steam. Don't want to *be them*. Don't recognise my face. I'm leaving her. I can't stay with her. Sick.

5

Living room.

GLORIA: What's this?
JARED: It's for.
GLORIA: A dress.
JARED: For your premiere.

She tries it on.

GLORIA: Can you. The zipper.

He does.

JARED: You look.
GLORIA: Old.
JARED: Beautiful. As the day we. Try the shoes.

She does. Stands in front of a mirror.

Suits you.

He stands behind her.

GLORIA: Thank you.

He kisses her neck.

You smell nice. You showered.
JARED: How was?
GLORIA: Didn't you shower at work? You always.
JARED: It was a rough day. And you? How was today? Better?
GLORIA: Do you feel guilty? Is the dress?
JARED: A what?

She takes the dress off. Stands in underwear. Unsteady.

GLORIA: You stink of her and you stink of blood.
JARED: Not in front.
GLORIA: Fucking stinks.

She tears the dress.

JARED: Stop.
PAUL: Mummy.
JARED: Paul go to your.
PAUL: Mummy.

PAUL *clings to* GLORIA.

PAUL: It's alright Mummy … Mummy …
GLORIA: Animal.

6

Living room. Recording device on table.

GLORIA: Thrilled to be working again. And the role. A dream. Which magazine was it?
MAN: The weekend. Colour. Thanks for inviting us into your home. Wow.
GLORIA: Do you want?

CASSIE *brings water.*

Water. Thanks Cassie. This is Cassie.
MAN: Hi Cassie.
CASSIE: Hi.
GLORIA: It's on right? You switched it on? [*Meaning the recording device*]
MAN: Yes I.
GLORIA: Because.
MAN: It's on.
GLORIA: She's a great help. Aren't you Cassie.

CASSIE *laughs faintly.*

Because there's nothing worse than half-way through you realise the fucking thing's not even on and all this talking for nothing.
MAN: It's on. See.
GLORIA: Cassie looks after Paul. Our son. You'll meet him.
MAN: Great, I'd like.
GLORIA: And sometimes my husband bends her over and fucks her.

Silence.

MAN: So. The role. How're you finding?
GLORIA: Great to work again. She's just a fuck.
CASSIE: Paul. Let's go play.
GLORIA: A godsend. Don't know what we'd do without. And yes the role. My God. She really.
MAN: Went through hell right? Locked away for how many years? Her own father. I mean that must. Jesus. How do you put yourself in her place? What's that like? Being inside her?

Silence.

GLORIA: Sorry. I.

Pause.

MAN: Do you bring her home?

GLORIA: Sorry?

MAN: You think about her all the time. That cellar. No light. No air. Damp. Disgusting. Jesus. And being back onstage. Nowhere to hide right?

GLORIA: Right. The role's a blessing and Dominic's just great, really supportive. Wants me to dig deep. Expose. Because this story. That poor girl. The father. Like an ape. Ruling his. Living out his. Hell. Absolute.

MAN: Like animals right. Her children. Speaking some kind of made-up language?

GLORIA: Their own, yes.

MAN: Horrific. And Dominic. Tell us.

GLORIA: He's one of a kind and we click. Yes there's conflict yes he infuriates me and no it's not always easy or fun but who needs *fun,* right? I like to be pushed and I want to go there and he makes things happen which I haven't found with other directors. Can't draw everything out of myself. Need his eye. Even if I make the occasional mistake. [*Laughter.*] He always knows when I need a push or something positive—a compliment—so we can go on.

MAN: Wow.

GLORIA: I only do what I do to please him.

Pause.

MAN: Right. We just need a few photos. This is Derek.

DEREK: Great place.

GLORIA: Thanks Derek. We're happy here.

DEREK: The view. Really lucky. Shall we?

They move to the balcony. DEREK *takes photos.*

GLORIA: Close to the sky. With my orange juice in the morning.

She's unsteady. Supports herself.

Almost touch it.

DEREK: That's great. Like that.

GLORIA: Like?

She poses.

DEREK: Good. Let me check. Good. More of that, Gloria.

She poses.

And to me.
GLORIA: The wind.
DEREK: Like that.
GLORIA: Have we met? Your face.
DEREK: No. I don't think.
GLORIA: Your face is very.
DEREK: But I'm a big fan. Don't move.

She doesn't move. He shoots.

That film where you. Italian. The island.
GLORIA: Long time ago.
DEREK: Beautifully shot.
GLORIA: We nearly?

Unsteady.

DEREK: Few inside.

They go in.

Sitting.

The sofa or the bed.

Good. Like that. Sexy. More of that.
GLORIA: I'm all yours, Derek.

Laughter.

DEREK: Keep it like. Good.
GLORIA: You like me, Derek?

Laughter.

Sorry.

Laughter.

DEREK: Is something?
GLORIA: You think I'm hot don't you.
DEREK: Gloria.
GLORIA: Derek.

Only she laughs now.

It's okay. Really.

Still laughing. Too much.

DEREK: Sorry. This.
GLORIA: You want a bit of this?

Her laughter. Suppresses.

Staring at me. With your fucking.
DEREK: Okay. That's.
GLORIA: Sorry. I'll be good now, a good girl … Derek.

Cracks up.

DEREK: This is not what.
GLORIA: What're you staring at fucking pig? You Derek fuck.

Silence.

MAN: Get a couple with the son.
CASSIE: Wait.

She brings PAUL. *Straightens his hair.*

MAN: Next to her.
CASSIE: Here Paul. Next to Mummy.

PAUL *sits next to* GLORIA. DEREK *shoots.*

DEREK: Good.
MAN: Both real serious.
DEREK: That's good.

Checks the display on his camera.

Nice and formal. Mother and son. Good.
MAN: Is she alright?
CASSIE: She's fine. Tired.
MAN: Okay. Couple more.

7

Living room.

CASSIE: They're cancelling—*postponing*—the premiere. She's a mess. They never know if she'll turn up, what state. Drunk, destructive. I'm worried about Paul. It's not right. His mother. She wants you back. She doesn't care what happened.

JARED: Cassie.

CASSIE: She actually thinks it'll still go ahead. She wants to wear the dress you gave her. She wants you there. On her arm afterwards. I'm sorry. Everything.

JARED: You looked so hot. In the mirror, in her new dress. It was nice but it meant nothing.

Pause.

I'll be back later to pick Paul up.

CASSIE: Heard you got promoted.

JARED: My own unit.

CASSIE: Congratulations.

JARED: Thank you.

8

Living room.

GLORIA *alone. The television.* PAUL *enters. In his pyjamas. Sleepy.*

PAUL: Can't sleep.

He cuddles up to her on the couch.

GLORIA: It's okay darling. Just lie here with Mummy.

PAUL: Who are they fighting?

GLORIA: Bad guys.

PAUL: I had nightmares.

GLORIA: It's okay, sweetheart.

PAUL: Fog. I couldn't see. I got lost, couldn't find our door.

GLORIA: You're safe now.

She cradles him.

9

Living room.

GLORIA: I saw you on TV. You both looked happy. Smiling for the cameras. Your new life. Congratulations. All those medals. Cassie was watching too. You know I think she felt something for you. That you actually *cared* for her. Poor girl.

JARED: Gloria.

GLORIA: You've done well. A general's daughter.

JARED: I want Paul to live with me and Jacinta. This is not a good environment for him.

GLORIA: Sometimes on television, there's a blast. Windows blown out. A building like ours. But it's not. Will the fighting be over soon?

JARED: Where is he?

GLORIA: With Cassie. In the park. We can.

Pause.

If you want.

He runs his fingers through her hair.

I won't tell.

They kiss.

You can do anything you want.

JARED: Gloria.

GLORIA: A what-do-you-call-it? Mercy fuck.

JARED: I.

GLORIA: Like when we first met. Except it hurts.

JARED: I want my son to come and live with me. I don't want him near you.

Silence.

We're finished. Do you understand?

She nods.

10

Living room.

PAUL *is playing his video game.* MADDIE *watches.*

PAUL: Want a go?

MADDIE: No thanks.

GLORIA *enters, carrying a present. She kisses* PAUL *on the head. He keeps playing his game.* GLORIA *stares at* MADDIE.

GLORIA: I don't know you.

MADDIE: I'm Maddie. Remember.

GLORIA: Maddie?

MADDIE: My mum, she.

GLORIA: [*screaming*] Cassie!

CASSIE *runs in.*

Who's she?

CASSIE: You remember Maddie. My daughter Maddie.

Pause.

No-one to look after her today so she's hanging out with me, right Maddie?

MADDIE: What's that? [*Meaning the present*]

CASSIE: Sweetheart come help Mum stack the dishwasher. We're going soon.

GLORIA: Oh this. For Paul.

CASSIE: Look darling, Mummy got you a present.

CASSIE *switches off the game.*

PAUL: What is it?

CASSIE: Open and see.

He just holds it in his hands and stares at it.

MADDIE: Open it.

PAUL *opens the present—the tin bird.*

GLORIA: You can make it fly.

PAUL *does nothing, just stares at the bird.*

You squeeze the handle. The wings. To make it fly.

He does.

[*To* CASSIE] His father is collecting him tomorrow. There's no more work for you here.

11

Living room.

Night. GLORIA *watching TV. Sound on mute.* PAUL *enters and sits beside her. Nothing for a long time, then she walks to the kitchen, opens the fridge, stares inside. Finally, she pours a glass of milk which he drinks, still watching the television. When he's finished, she rinses the glass and puts it in the dishwasher. She takes a long, sharp kitchen knife from the drawer and sits back down.* PAUL *snuggles into her. She strokes his hair. They watch television. She cradles him, kisses his head. Stares at the television.*

GLORIA: He's out there. In the dust and green light. In rooms where terrified people cover their heads. Like this—

She demonstrates.

Dead eyes. Sex. Perfume.

Pause.

Once he held her and whispered *my queen*. The boy their everything. His breath is hot against her neck. Little chest rising, falling. The kitchen knife is a splinter of ice in her hand. Her thoughts crowd around it. She's doing this. Because she loves him. Calm now. A slice. Listen. Air sucked from room. Little body heavier. Lays him down. Kisses his eyes. Full of love.

She lays him down and closes his eyes.

12

Living room.

PAUL*'s body is put in a body bag by* POLICE OFFICERS. *A* FORENSIC OFFICER *takes photos of the scene.*

13

Empty stage.

GLORIA: I stand upstage of the curtain. Listening to the audience. That hum. Does it even have a name? The house lights dim. Silence.

Fade.

▼ ▼ ▼ ▼ ▼

FIVE

1

Family room.

MADDIE *is nursing a newborn baby.*

DEREK: Ready sweetheart?

Laughter.

MADDIE: You start.

Laughter.

DEREK: No, you.

Laughter.

MADDIE: [*quietly*] Oh look. We woke her up. Hello. Hello little one.

Pause.

No. Actually, we don't go down there much.

DEREK: Not anymore. No.

MADDIE: Not safe.

DEREK: Nah, not really safe.

Pause.

Totally happy here. Yep. Everything we need. Each other.

Laughter.

MADDIE: Got it all. Her.

DEREK: Each other. The view.

MADDIE: Out there with my orange juice. Close to the sky. Who'd want to live down there?

DEREK: People look up and want what we've got. The view. Clean. Safe.

MADDIE: We're lucky.

DEREK: It's different from where other people live. More comfortable. And higher up.

Laughter.

MADDIE: [*to the baby*] Hello. Mummy's little girl. Say hello.
DEREK: Where's Paul? Paul. Paul.
MADDIE: Yes. Terrible. Her own. I can't bear to.
DEREK: We don't.
MADDIE: How any mother.
DEREK: Didn't hear a thing, no. [*Calling*] Paul. Dinner.

2

Paul's room.

PAUL: I walk room to room. No-one shoots back. No-one's screaming. It's calm. I place the shots wherever I like. Head or body. Leg if I want them to fall first. So I don't get bored. So each kill doesn't feel the same.

3

Studio.

CASSIE: [*smiling*] Like this?
ASSISTANT DIRECTOR: They want more smile.

CASSIE *smiles more.*

Think about the people at home.
CASSIE: Huh?
ASSISTANT DIRECTOR: On their sofas. Eating dinner. Teeth. Smile.

CASSIE *stares and smiles.*

Happy happy. Warm inside. Twirling the ribbons. Good. And—we're done.
CASSIE: How was it?
ASSISTANT DIRECTOR: Great. Hold on, they need one more. Okay, you're putting the packet in the trolley. You've made your decision. You're happy. You love life. You made the right decision and your family will love you for it. Good Cassie. Okay down the barrel and smile.

CASSIE *smiles.*

Good. That's it. Good girl.

4

Ship cabin.

JARED: I look back to shore. The harbour. Black mirror. Lights. Everyone wants to live up there now. Close to sky. I've forgotten them. Don't even dream them. Then I'm walking the streets of some city, in the crowd or shop window, her face, a split second ghostly gone again, or I'm fucking a woman I paid to love me in some port and suddenly her face is right there.

Silence.

On the TV fixed to the wall of my cabin, a woman is crying. News or documentary. She's in jail. One of those tables you know with the glass. Sound mute. I can't stop staring. Her face is a cavern. I need to sleep. Tonight I'll sleep. Jesus. Her face.

5

Cell.

GLORIA: You want me to describe how it felt. At you or the camera? Not my best. At you. Like a conversation. Okay. Like this? Music. Listen. What? Sorry. Yes of course I'm ready.

Her face.

Slow fade.

THE END

GRIFFIN THEATRE COMPANY PRESENTS
THE WORLD PREMIERE OF

GLORIA
BY BENEDICT ANDREWS
26 AUGUST - 8 OCTOBER

Director Lee Lewis
Associate Director Ben Winspear
Designer Sophie Fletcher
Lighting Designer Luiz Pampolha
Audio Visual Designer Toby Knyvett
Composer Steve Toulmin
Photographer & Videographer Brett Boardman
Stage Manager Natalie Moir
Production Coordinator Danny Oliver
Child Chaperone Elishia Semaan
With Chloe Bayliss, Kristy Best, Marta Dusseldorp, Louis Fontaine, Huw Higginson, Max Philips, Pierce Wilcox, Meyne Wyatt

SBW STABLES THEATRE
26 AUGUST - 8 OCTOBER

Production Sponsor

AV Sponsor

Government Partners

Griffin acknowledges the generosity of the Seaborn, Broughton and Walford Foundation in allowing it the use of the SBW Stables Theatre rent free, less outgoings, since 1986.

PLAYWRIGHT'S NOTE

In the final scene of Michelangelo Antonioni's psychedelic masterpiece *Zabriskie Point* (1970), a house in the Arizona desert explodes in slow motion. While Pink Floyd warbles away on the soundtrack, Antonioni shows various domestic objects – racks of clothes, outdoor dining set, fridge, colour TV etc. – blown to smithereens. Slowed right down, the destruction of these objects is hypnotic, exquisite and sublime – like abstract expressionist paintings seen on acid, or satellite images of deep space. As Pink Floyd fades out, Antonioni cuts to the blissed-out face of a young hippie woman. For her, and for Antonioni, the destruction is a gesture of ecstatic liberation. I had these repeated detonations in mind while writing *Gloria*.

My play explodes domestic drama into something prismatic, crystalline and kaleidoscopic. Realities overlap, shift and entwine, like when a Skype call breaks down into dancing pixels – which, by the way, look not unlike those slow motion explosions in *Zabriskie Point*. Boundaries between dream and life, reality and fantasy, actor and role become porous, unreliable.

Gloria contains five parts, conceived of as five separate yet interlocking plays-within-plays. The characters generally keep their names as they move across each play, but their roles shift, like Chinese Whispers. In Part One, for example, Jared is Gloria's teenage son, in Part Three, he's her co-actor backstage at a theatre, in Part Four, he's her soon to be ex-husband, and in Part Five, a sailor in the hull of a freighter. Only Gloria keeps her role – that of an actress – across the play's five parts. The play whirls around her, like the particles of that exploding house or pixels breaking apart during a Skype call.

Gloria is full of echoes, mirror realities, distorted harmonies. It digs into the borderline condition of being an actor. Night after night, onstage, we ask actors to play out experiences which, in everyday life, would send us to the madhouse or jail. Actors are like our emotional guinea pigs, researching the limits of human behaviour. They must possess the boundless play of children, the frenzied imagination of a poet, the forensic mind of a detective, as well as gigantic hearts. *Gloria* depicts an actress in the grip of an emotional breakdown. Like Myrtle Gordon, the character played by Gena Rowlands in John Cassavetes' film *Opening Night* (1977), she experiences a total collapse of role and life. The slipping boundaries between role and life influence the form of the play itself. *Gloria* is a kind of demented love song to the theatre and to actresses in particular.

Benedict Andrews
Writer

DIRECTOR'S NOTE

If I could have one wish it would be to go forward in time about 400 years in order to get enough perspective on this age to know what is actually happening to the world right now.

As Juno arrives at Jupiter and takes photos of the moons that got Galileo into so much trouble, as Pokémon GO invades our streets, as suicide bombers and mad men with guns strip away any illusion of safety around the world, as Britain prepares to leave the EU under the leadership of a new Prime Minister, as the world contemplates the possibility of a President Trump, as one woman a week dies a victim of domestic violence in Australia, it feels almost impossible to know if we are in the middle of a 200 year war or nearing the end of a 100 year war.

Gloria may well be a love song to the great women who act on our stages, who we call upon to embody the imaginative state of our nation. But the play is also a symptom of the time we are in ... a greedy time, a selfish, self-centred, vain, fearful, frantic, unstable time in which we cling so hard to anything that can make us feel connected to other people, anything that can feel real. *Gloria* is not a portrait of an actor, it is a portrait of us, one we are desperately trying to deny. Sometimes it takes an Australian on the other side of the planet to have enough distance to see us for what we are becoming.

Lee Lewis
Director

Benedict Andrews

Playwright

Benedict Andrews is one of Australia's most sought-after theatre practitioners, with his talents crossing numerous creative disciplines. His previous credits as playwright include: for Belvoir: *Every Breath*. Benedict has adapted a number of stage works himself or with colleagues, and directed their premiere productions. These credits include: for Sydney Theatre Company (STC): *Life is a Dream* with Beatrix Christian (after Calderón), *The Maids* with Andrew Upton (after Genet), *Three Sisters* with Beatrix Christian (after Chekhov) and *The War of the Roses* with Tom Wright (after Shakespeare), which won six Helpmann Awards including Best Play and Best Direction of a Play and five Sydney Theatre Awards including Best Mainstage Production; for Belvoir: *The Seagull* (after Chekhov); and for Young Vic (London): *Three Sisters* (after Chekhov), for which he was awarded the 2012 London Critics Circle Award for Best Director. Benedict's directing credits are extensive, both in Australia and abroad. Some of his national credits include: for Belvoir: *The Chairs, A Midsummer Night's Dream* and *Measure for Measure*, which was awarded Best Direction, Best Stage Design and Best Mainstage Play at the 2010 Sydney Theatre Awards, *The Threepenny Opera* and *Who's Afraid of Virginia Woolf?*; for State Theatre Company of South Australia (STCSA) whilst Artistic Director of Magpie 2 Theatre: *Features of Blown Youth, In the Solitude of the Cotton Fields* and *Mercedes*; for STC, where Benedict was Resident Director from 2000 to 2003: *Attempts On Her Life, The City, Endgame, Far Away, Fireface, Gross Und Klein*, which, after winning the 2011 Helpmann Award for Best Direction, played to great acclaim at Théâtre de la Ville in Paris, The Barbican in London, the Wiener Festwochen in Vienna and the Ruhrfestspiele in Recklinghausen, *Julius Caesar, La Dispute, Mr Kolpert, Old Masters* and *The Season At Sarsaparilla,* which was awarded the Green Room Award for Best Director in 2009. Internationally, Benedict has directed productions for the following companies: The Almeida (London), English National Opera (where he directed the Olivier-nominated *Caligula*), The Komische Opera (Berlin), National Theatre (Reykjavik), Oper Frankfurt, Royal Danish Opera, the Schaubühne am Lehniner Platz (Berlin), the Young Vic (London) and St Ann's Warehouse (New York). In 1998 Benedict was awarded the Gloria Payten and Gloria Dawn Foundation Fellowships, and in 2005 he won the Sydney Myer Performing Arts Award. This year, Benedict's first book of poems for Pitt Street Poetry, *Lens Flare*, won the 2016 Mary Gilmore Award; a collected volume of his plays will be published by Oberon Books; and Benedict's first feature film, *Una*, starring Rooney Mara and Ben Mendelsohn will be released around the world.

Lee Lewis

Director

Lee is the Artistic Director of Griffin Theatre Company and one of Australia's leading directors. For Griffin she has directed: *The Bleeding Tree*, for which Lee was awarded Best Director at the 2016 Helpmann Awards, *Eight Gigabytes of Hardcore Pornography, Masquerade* (co-directed with Sam Strong), *Emerald City, A Rabbit for Kim Jong-il, The Serpent's Table* (co-directed with Darren Yap), *Replay, Silent Disco, The Bull, The Moon and the Coronet of Stars, The Call, A Hoax* and *The Nightwatchman*; for Griffin and Bell Shakespeare: *The Literati*; for Bell Shakespeare: *The School for Wives* and *Twelfth Night*; for Belvoir: *That Face, This Heaven, Half and Half, A Number, 7 Blowjobs* and *Ladybird*; for MTC: David Williamson's *Rupert*, which toured to Washington DC as part of the World Stages International Arts Festival and to Sydney's Theatre Royal in 2014; for STC: *Honour, Love-Lies-Bleeding* and *ZEBRA!*; for Darwin Festival: *Highway of Lost Hearts*; for the National Institute of Dramatic Art (NIDA): *Big Love, Shopping and Fucking, After Dinner* and *The Winter's Tale*; and for the Western Australian Academy of Performing Arts (WAAPA): *As You Like It.*

Ben Winspear

Associate Director

Ben is Griffin's current Associate Artist. He was formerly Resident Director at STC where, along with running Wharf 2 as a new writing space, his credits in directing premiere productions include: *Metamorphosis, These People, Morph, This Little Piggy* and *Thyestes*. Other directing credits include: for Downstairs Belvoir: *Silver*; for NIDA: *Saved*; for STC: *King Lear, Macbeth, The Tempest*; for the University of New South Wales: *Insect, Monkey* and *Pantagleize*; and as Co-Director: for STC: *Victory*.

Sophie Fletcher

Designer

Sophie's theatre credits include, as Set and Costume Designer: for Griffin: *Caress/Ache, Emerald City*; for Griffin and Bell Shakespeare: *The Literati*; for Belvoir: *This Heaven*; and for Pantsguys / ATYP: *Sweet Nothings*. As Design Assistant: for Belvoir: *Babyteeth, Every Breath, Peter Pan*; for MTC: *Miss Julie*; for Opera Australia: *The Marriage of Figaro, The Ring Cycle*; and for Sydney Theatre Company: *Gross und Klein, The Maids, Waiting for Godot*. Her film credits include, as Costume Designer: for Whitefalk Films: *Florence Has Left the Building*; as Production Designer: for Whitefalk Films: *Shadow Self*; and as Production and Costume Designer: for Whitefalk Films: *How to Get Clean.*

Luiz Pampolha

Lighting Designer

Luiz is a graduate of NIDA, and a member of the Illuminating Engineering Society of Australia and New Zealand. Some of his lighting design credits include: for Griffin: *The Call, Concussion, Emerald City, The Kid, The Nightwatchman, A Rabbit for Kim Jong-il, The Serpent's Table, The Story Of The Miracles At Cookie's Table*; for Australian Chamber Orchestra (ACO): *Kreutzer vs Kreutzer*; for Bell Shakespeare: *Twelfth Night*, for which Luiz was nominated for a Green Room Award; for Belvoir: *Antigone, Brothers Wreck, Don't Take Your Love To Town, This Heaven, Ruben Guthrie*; for Inscription in association with B Sharp: *Love*, for which Luiz was nominated for a Sydney Theatre Award for Best Lighting; for Marguerite Pepper Productions: *Happy As Larry*; for Pinchgut Opera: *Castor et Pollux, The Chimney Sweep, Griselda*; for Sydney Chamber Opera: *The Cunning Little Vixen*; for Sydney Opera House: *The CODA Collective, danceTank, Emergence*; and for STC: *The 7 Stages of Grieving, Hip, Love-Lies-Bleeding*, for which Luiz was nominated for a Sydney Theatre Award, *Rabbit, The Removalists, Romeo & Juliet, Saturn's Return* and *Waiki.*

Toby Knyvett

Audio Visual Designer

Toby Knyvett is an award-winning video and interactive artist. His previous video and lighting design credits for the stage include: for CDP: *Incredible Book Eating Boy*; for Next Wave Festival: *The River Eats*, which was remounted at the National Museum of Modern and Contemporary Art (Korea); for Performance Space: *I Might Blow Up Someday* with queer performance trio Hissy Fit; and for Sport For Jove: *All's Well That Ends Well*, which won Toby the Sydney Theatre Critic Award for Best Lighting Design (Independent Production). Lighting design credits include: for the Australian National Maritime Museum: *Actions Stations*, which saw Toby light the HMAS Onslow submarine and HMAS Vampire destroyer. Interactive art credits as Creator and/or Developer include: for the Sydney Opera House's 'Creative Play' program: *Echo Tables*, in which participants collaboratively draw with their shadows, and *The Unbroken Line*, a 7.5m wide 'bodyscreen' that reacts to movements without touch. Toby's current project, *Orbital Illumination*, aims to reflect unused sunlight in space down to earth using mirrors.

Steve Toulmin

Composer

Steve's credits as Composer and/or Sound Designer include: for Griffin: *Beached, The Bleeding Tree*; for Griffin and La Boîte Theatre Company: *Hoax*; for Bell Shakespeare: *Othello*; for Belvoir: *The Blind Giant Is Dancing, Blue Wizard, Ivanov, Is This Thing On?, Jasper Jones, La Traviata, Scorched, The Seed* and *20 Questions*; for Ensemble Theatre: *Circle Mirror Transformation, Great Falls, Liberty Equality Fraternity*; for La Boîte Theatre Company: *Hamlet, Julius Caesar, Tender Napalm*; for La Boîte Theatre Company and STC: *Edward Gant's Amazing Feats of Loneliness*; for Michael Sieders Presents and Griffin Independent: *Porn. Cake*; for the Royal Queensland Show: *Arena Spectacular*; for QTC: *That Face, Switzerland*: for Sydney Festival: *All The Sex I've Ever Had*; for STC: *Little Mercy*; and for Strut & Fret: *Blanc De Blanc*. As Foley Artist, Steve has worked on: for STC: *Our Town*. Steve's previous credits as Audio Visual Designer include: for Griffin: *Angela's Kitchen, Between Two Waves*; and for STC: *God of Carnage, Tot Mom*. Steve is also known as a songwriter and music producer, having worked with artists such as Ricki-Lee Coulter, Samantha Jade and Megan Washington.

Brett Boardman

Photographer / Videographer

Brett Boardman is a photographer based in Sydney. He works across the disciplines of architectural, landscape, portrait and performance photography, with his work being published world-wide. Brett's works are held in the Museum of Sydney, The National Portrait Gallery of Australia, The State Library of NSW and Tweed River Gallery as well as in private collections. His recent international exhibitions include: *The Pool* at the Venice Architecture Biennale (Venice, 2016); *Mono No Aware* at Japan Foundation Sydney (Sydney, 2015); and *ENERGY: Oil and Post-oil Architecture and Grids* at MAXXI Gallery (Rome, 2013). Brett's previous credits as Audio Visual Designer include: for Belvoir: *2000 Feet Away*. Brett was a finalist for the 2011, 2013 and 2015 Olive Cotton Biennial Award for Excellence in Photographic Portraiture, and won the Australian Professional Photographer of the Year at the Canon AIPP Awards in 2005.

Chloe Bayliss

Maddie / Girl

Chloe Bayliss works in both performing and creative capacities across drama and dance in Australia. Her previous acting credits include: for Ensemble Theatre: *Charitable Intent, Circle Mirror Transformation*, for which she was nominated for Best Supporting Actress at the GLUG Theatre Awards, *The Good Doctor, Rapture Blister Burn*; and for Red Line Productions: *The Whale*. Chloe's film credits include: *Backtrack*, which screened at Tribeca Film Festival; and *Driftwood Dustmites,* which was nominated for the Generations 14plus Award at the 2015 Berlinale. Chloe's TV credits include: for the ABC: *Dance Academy*; for Channel 10: *Reef Doctors*; for Foxtel: *Deadly Women* (Season 7); and for Nine Network: *Doctor Doctor*. Chloe was thrilled to be nominated as a finalist in the 2016 Heath Ledger Scholarship. Chloe is a proud member of Actors Equity, a patron of the Hunter & Northern Kidney Association (HANKA) and an Ambassador for the Red Cross Blood Service.

Kristy Best

Cassie / Woman

This is Kristy's debut with Griffin. Her previous stage credits include: for ATYP and Raw Hide: *Alaska*; for Newtown Theatre: *Nothing Like Old Times*; for Powerhouse Youth Theatre: *She Loves Me, She Loves Me Not*; and for Q Theatre Company: *Truck Stop*. Kristy has featured on screen in a number of independent short and feature-length films. Her television credits include: for ABC: *Sunday Best*; for Nine Network: *Here Come the Habibs*; for Network Ten: *Neighbours*; for SBS: *Fat Pizza, Legally Brown* (Season 2) and *East West 101*; and for Seven Network: *Home and Away.*

Marta Dusseldorp

Gloria

Marta Dusseldorp is one of our country's most skilled and versatile actors, with a career spanning more than two decades across Australian stage, film and television. Marta has worked with many major theatre companies in Australia, stand-out productions including: for Griffin and STC: *Like a Fishbone*; for Belvoir: *Cloudstreet*; for Malthouse Theatre Company: *Journal of the Plague Year*; for MTC: *Three Sisters*; for STC: *The Lost Echo* and *War of the Roses*, for which Marta received a Helpmann Award in 2009. Film credits include: *Burning Man, Innocence, Paradise Road* and *Praise*. Marta has worked extensively in Australian television. She has just completed filming the much-anticipated fourth season of *A Place to Call Home*, while the second season of *Janet King* has just aired, in which she plays the title role and for which she won the AACTA Award for Best Leading Actress in 2015. Marta's telemovie credits include: *After the Deluge, BlackJack, Devil's Dust, Hell Has Harbour Views* and *Jack Irish: Bad Debts, Black Tide* and *Dead Point.*

Louis Fontaine

Paul

At 13 years of age, Louis Fontaine has already appeared in an array of stage works. His previous credits include: for Griffin and STCSA: *Masquerade* (Sydney Opera House season and national tour); for Bonnie Lythgoe Productions: *Snow White*; for Chugg Entertainment: *Robbie Williams: The Swing Tour*; for Gordon Frost Organisation: *The Sound of Music*; for Opera Australia: *Carmen*; and for Packemin Productions: *The Wizard of Oz*. Louis attends Brent Street, and apart from his work on stage, has appeared in various television commercials, music videos and charity events for organisations such as the Starlight Foundation.

Huw Higginson

Derek / Man

Huw has worked consistently in television, film and theatre since his training at The London Academy of Dramatic Art. Previous stage credits include: for Griffin: *The House on the Lake*, for which Huw won a GLUG award for Most Outstanding Performance by an Actor in a Leading Role; for pantsguys and Griffin Independent: *On the Shore of the Wide World*; for CDP: *Lone Star, Mr Stink*; for Christine Harris & HIT Productions: *Love Letters*; for Criterion Theatre (West End): *What the Butler Saw*; for Hampstead Theatre: *Abigail's Party*; for MTC: *Great Expectations*; for Middle Ground Theatre Company: *Meeting Joe Strummer*; for Octagon Theatre Bolton: *All My Sons, Comedians, And Did Those Feet, Demolition Man, The Winslow Boy, A Streetcar Named Desire*, for which Huw was nominated for a MEN Award for Best Supporting Actor; for PW Productions: *Arsenic and Old Lace*; and for Rio Tint and Hampstead Theatre; *In the Club*. Huw's television credits include: for ABC: *Hiding, Miss Fisher's Murder Mysteries, Rake* (Season 4), *Secret River*; for Channel 10: *Mary: Making of a Princess*; for Foxtel: *Deadline Gallipoli, Secret City*; and for Seven: *Home and Away*; for BBCTV: *Big Deal, Blessed, By Any Means, Living It, Casualty, Doctors, EastEnders, Holby City, Railway Murders, The Sarah Jane Adventures*; for Channel 4: *Peep Show*; and for ITV Network: *The Bill*, in which Huw featured as PC George Garfield in over 600 episodes spanning ten years, *The Giblets* and *Heartbeat*.

Max Philips

Paul

Gloria is Max's mainstage debut. Max's previous stage experience includes: for Sydney Grammar Edgecliff Prep School: *Rikki Tikki Tavi*. Max has also gained experience from and enjoyed success in Sydney regional speech and drama competitions, such as: Wollongong and Sydney Eisteddfods (2013-2016): Actors Championship, Character Solo, News Reading/Radio Announcing, Prose Speaking and Verse Speaking. Max's training includes drama workshops and short courses with ATYP and NIDA. Along with the dramatic arts, Max enjoys public speaking and debating, playing the trumpet, listening to old BBC radio shows, and playing sport – especially football, tennis, cricket and golf.

Pierce Wilcox

Client / Man 2 / Kip / Assistant Director

Pierce has created work across a multitude of dramatic forms, utilising his array of skills as an artist. Pierce's theatre credits include: as Co-Creator/Performer: for Belvoir Downstairs: *They've Already Won*; for Sekrit Projekt: *Only You Can Save Us*; as Librettist: for Carriageworks and Sydney Chamber Opera (SCO): *Fly Away Peter*; for SCO: *Notes from Underground*; and for the 20th Biennale of Sydney and SCO: *Victory over the Sun* (which Pierce also directed). Pierce's other creative credits include: as Director: for NIDA: *Caligula*; for Somersault Theatre Company: *My Name is Truda Vitz*; for the University of Sydney: *Agamemnon*; and for 107 Projects: *Great Island,* which Pierce adapted from Marivaux's *L'Île des esclaves*; as Assistant Director: for Darlinghurst Theatre Company: *All My Sons*; for NIDA: *Story of the Red Mountains*; and as Dramaturg: for NIDA: *Hinterland* and *Choreography*; and for True West Theatre: *The Westlands*. Pierce was the Affiliate Director for Griffin in 2013, which saw him assistant direct *The Floating World*. He is currently the Associate Artist at SCO.

Meyne Wyatt

Jared

A graduate of NIDA, Meyne has worked extensively in leading roles on both stage and screen. Meyne's stage credits include: for Griffin: *Silent Disco*; for Savage Productions, Michael Sieders and Griffin Independent: *The Brothers Size*; for Bell Shakespeare: *School for Wives*; for Belvoir: *Buried City* and *Peter Pan*, which toured to the New Victory Theater (New York); for QTC: *Black Diggers*; and for STC: *Bloodland* and *King Lear*. Meyne's film credits include: *The Sapphires, The Turning* and *Strangerland*. On Australian television Meyne's credits include: for ABC: *Black Comedy, The Broken Shore* (telemovie) and *Redfern Now*, for which Meyne was nominated for The Graham Kennedy Award for Best Newcomer at the 2014 Logie Awards, the 2014 Equity Ensemble Award and the 2014 AACTA Award for Best Actor; and for Network 10: *Neighbours*, in which Meyne was a series regular.

ABOUT GRIFFIN THEATRE COMPANY

For nearly 40 years, Griffin has been dedicated to bringing the best Australian stories to the stage. We have a passion for developing Australian talent, with many of our nation's most celebrated artists starting their professional careers with us.

Griffin is a major force in shaping the future of Australian theatre: it is a home for the courageous and the curious, for the imaginations that inspire us. Iconic Australian stories such as *Lantana, The Boys, Holding the Man* and *The Heartbreak Kid* had their world premieres at Griffin.

Griffin produces an annual subscription season of four to five Main Season shows by Australian playwrights, and co-presents a season of new work with leading independent artists and special events from producers around the country. We also support artists through professional development opportunities, artist residencies and masterclasses.

Our home is the historic SBW Stables Theatre, Sydney's most intimate and engaging space for writers, actors and audiences to meet. We hope to see you here soon.

GRIFFIN THEATRE COMPANY
13 CRAIGEND ST
KINGS CROSS NSW 2011

02 9332 1052
INFO@GRIFFINTHEATRE.COM.AU
GRIFFINTHEATRE.COM.AU

SBW STABLES THEATRE
10 NIMROD ST
KINGS CROSS NSW 2011

BOOKINGS
GRIFFINTHEATRE.COM.AU
02 9361 3817

STAFF

Patron
Seaborn, Broughton and Walford Foundation

Griffin acknowledges the generosity of the Seaborn, Broughton and Walford Foundation in allowing it the use of the SBW Stables Theatre rent free, less outgoings, since 1986.

Board
Bruce Meagher (Chair), Tim Duggan, Patrick Guerrera, Lee Lewis, Kate Mulvany, Mario Philippou, Sue Procter, Lenore Robertson, Simone Whetton

Artistic Director & CEO
Lee Lewis

Associate Artist
Ben Winspear

General Manager
Karen Rodgers

Associate Producer - Programming
Melanie Carolan

Associate Producer - Development
Will Harvey

Associate Producer - Marketing
Estelle Conley

Publicist
Dino Dimitridis

Communications Associate
Aurora Scott

Marketing & Administration Coordinator
Lane Pitcher

Strategic Insights Consultant
Peter O'Connell

Production Manager
Kirby Brierty

Production Coordinator
Daniel Barber

Financial Consultant
Tracey Whitby

Finance Manager
Kylie Richards

Customer Relations Manager
Elliott Wilshier

Box Office Coordinator
Nicola James

Front of House Manager
Damien Storer

Front of House
Renee Heys, Julian Larnach, Kristina Paraschos

Studio Artists
Sofya Gollan, Catherine Fargher & Heather Grace Jones, Sheridan Harbridge, Phil Spencer

Writers Under Commission
Mary Rachel Brown
Declan Greene

Web Developer
Holly

Brand and Graphic Design
RE:

Cover Photography
Brett Boardman

GRIFFIN DONORS

Income from Griffin activities covers less than 40% of our operating costs – leaving an ever increasing gap for us to fill through government funding, sponsorship and the generosity of our individual supporters. Your support helps us bridge the gap and keep ticket prices affordable and our work at its best. To make a donation and a difference, contact Griffin on 9332 1052 or donate online at griffintheatre.com.au

Season Donors

Studio Program
Gil Appleton
James Emmett & Peter Wilson
Limb Family Foundation
Peter Graves
Ken & Lilian Horler
Sophie McCarthy
& Antony Green
Rhonda McIver
Geoff & Wendy Simpson
Danielle Smith

Commission $12,500+
Darin Cooper Foundation
Anthony & Suzanne
Maple-Brown

Main Stage Donor
$5,000 - $10,000
Peter Graves
Abraham James
Don & Leslie Parsonage
Sue Procter
The Robertson Family
Foundation
The Sky Foundation
Merilyn Sleigh
& Raoul de Ferranti

Workshop Donor
$1,000-$4,999
Anonymous (5)
Dr Gae Anderson
Stewart Baxter
Ellen Borda
Jane Bridge
Alex Byrne & Sue Hearn
Corinne Campbell
& Bryan Everts
Richard Cottrell
Mark Coulter
Tim Duggan
Ros & Paul Espie
John & Libby Fairfax
Westpac Foundation
Jono Gavin
Tina & Maurice Green
Larry & Tina Grumley
Judge Joe Harman
James Hartwright
& Kerrin D'Arcy
Libby Higgin
Margaret Johnston
Richard &
Elizabeth Longes
Sophie McCarthy
& Antony Green
Elaine & Bill McLaughlin
Bruce Meagher
& Greg Waters
Ruth Melville
Stephen Mills
Jo Nolan
Martin Portus
Pip Rath & Wayne Lonergan
Chris Reed
Crispin Rice
Amanda & Michael Solomon
Mike Thompson
Jane Thorn
Adrian Wiggins
& Siobhan Toohill
Paul & Jennifer Winch
Penny Young & Ian Neuss

Reading Donor $500-$999
Anonymous (4)
Wendy Ashton
Melissa Ball
Angela Bowne
Bernard Coles
Bryony & Tim Cox
Fiona Dewar
Max Dingle
Vicki Ditcham
Wendy Elder
Sheba Greenberg
Jennifer Hagan
Jacqueline Hayes
Angela Herscovitch
Michael Hobbs
Susan Hyde
C John Keightley
Daniel Knight
John Lam-Po-Tang
Jennifer Ledgar & Bob Lim
Rebecca Macfarling
& Paul Warnes
Lisa Manchur
Carina Martin
Christopher McCabe
John McCallum
Stuart McLean
Dr Steve McNamara
Dr Wendy Michaels
Anthony Paull
Steve & Belinda Rankine
Alex Oonagh Redmond
Annabel Ritchie
Karen Rodgers & Bill Harris
Natalie Shea
Diana Simmonds
Catherine Sullivan and
Alexandra Bowen
Isla Tooth
Judy & Sam Weiss
Simone Whetton

First Draft Donor
$200-$499
Anonymous (4)
Priscilla Adey
Jes Andersen
Robyn Ayres
Anna Barker
Pamela Bennett
Ronald Blair
Michaela Boland
Julie Bridgo
Rob Brookman & Verity
Laughton
Wendy Buswell
Amanda Clark
Bryan Cutler
Eric Dole & Mary Stollery
Susan Donnelly
Claire Evans
Elizabeth Evatt
Michael & Kerrie Eyers
Matt Garrett
Brenda Gottsche
Janet Grant
Elizabeth Hanley
Will Harvey & Ester Harding
Belinda Hazelton
John Head
Janet Heffernan
Mary Holt

PRODUCTION DONORS

You made this.

Production donors make a direct contribution to the costs of staging an individual play, chosen for its unique voice and the strength, insight and candour it brings to the stage. For more information, please contact our Development Manager on 9332 1052

Ladies Day 2016

Production Patrons
Robert Dick
& Erin Shiel
Reay McGuinness
Richard McHugh
& Kate Morgan
Bruce Meagher
& Greg Waters
Richard Weinstein
& Richard Benedict

Production Partners
Cambridge Events
Michael Hobbs
Steve Riethoff
Annabel Ritchie
Diana Simmonds
Jenny & Peter Solomon

The Bleeding Tree 2015

Presenting Partner
Gil Appleton

Production Patrons
Peter Brereton
Robert Dick
Richard McHugh
& Kate Morgan
Richard Weinstein

Production Partners
Tina & Maurice Green
Jon & Katie King
Bruce Meagher
& Greg Waters
John Mitchell
Rachel Procter
Steve Riethoff
Simone Whetton
Carole & David Yuile

Val Jory
Maria & Ross Kelly
Carolyn Lowry
Ian & Elizabeth MacDonald
Rob Macfarlan
& Nicole Abadee
Stephen Manning
Patrick McIntyre
Duncan McKay
Nicole McKenna
Kent Carrington McPhee
Keith Miller
Sarah Miller
Stephen Mills
Neville Mitchell
Kate Mulvany
Kerry O'Kane
Annie Page & Colin Fletcher
Christopher Powell
Bill Roberts
Ann Rocca
Rebecca Rocheford Davies
Ellen & Trevor Rodgers
Peter Rooke
Catherine Rothery
Gemma Rygate
Julianne Schultz
Roger Sewell
Jann Skinner
Leigh Small
Rob Spence
Geoffrey Starr
Augusta Supple
Sue Thomson
Benson Waghorn
Arisa Yura
William Zappa
Aviva Ziegler

We would also like to thank Peter O'Connell for his expertise, guidance and time.

Current as of 8 June, 2016

GRIFFIN FUND

The Griffin Fund is a new initiative focusing on education programs, leadership pathways for artists, touring Griffin productions and international exchange opportunities. Donations to the Fund are pledged for a three-year period. It is an investment in the future prospects of the company and the artists we work with. For more information please visit griffintheatre.com.au/support-us or contact our Development Manager on 9332 1052.

Griffin Fund Donors
Baly Douglas Foundation
John Bell & Anna Volska
Nathan Bennett & Yael Perry
Michael & Charmaine Bradley
Ange Cecco & Melanie Bienemann
Alison Deans & Kevin Powell
Catherine Dovey & Kim Williams
Lilian & Ken Horler
Peter Ingle
Kiong Lee & Richard Funston
Lee Lewis & Brett Boardman
Sophie McCarthy & Antony Green
Bruce Meagher & Greg Waters
Dr David Nguyen
Peter & Dianne O'Connell
Rebel Penfold-Russell
Ian Phipps
Ian Robertson
Augusta Supple
Will Sheehan
Stuart Thomas
Simon Wellington & Sanjeev Kumar
Carole & David Yuile

PORTRAIT OF A CHARACTER ARTISTS

Chris Antico
Angus Callander
Max Cullen
James Hancock
Jasper Knight
Emma Magenta
Caroline McLean-Foldes
Michael McIntyre
James Patradoon
Nicola Scott
Rachael Szalay
Samantha Tidbeck
Edwina White

GRIFFIN SPONSORS

Griffin would like to thank the following:

Government Supporters

Patron

2016 Season Sponsor

Production Sponsors

Foundations and Trusts

GIRGENSOHN FOUNDATION

Company Lawyers

Associate Sponsor

Company Sponsors

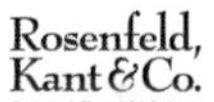

DESIGNKINGCOMPANY

Griffin Theatre Company is assisted by the Australian Government through the Australia Council, its arts funding and advisory body; and the NSW Government through Arts NSW.